STAMP COLLECTING

PHILATELIC TERMS ILLUSTRATED

JAMES MACKAY

D1613348

STANLEY GIBBONS PUBLICATIONS LTD LONDON AND RINGWOOD

Published by Stanley Gibbons Publications Ltd
Editorial, Sales Offices and Distribution Centre:
5 Parkside, Christchurch Road, Ringwood,
Hants BH24 3SH

© *Stanley Gibbons Publications Ltd 1987*

Philatelic Terms Illustrated—initially compiled by
Russell Bennett and James Watson—was first published
as a part-work in Gibbons *Stamp Monthly* in 1970–2.
First published in book form, 1973, second edition
1978. Third edition 1987.

Also in Stanley Gibbons Stamp Collecting Series:
Stamp Collecting—How to Start
Stamp Collecting—How to Identify Stamps
Stamp Collecting—Collecting by Theme
*Stamp Collecting—How to Arrange and Write-up a Stamp
                Collection*
Stamp Collecting—A Guide to Modern Philately

*Text pages designed by Julia Lilauwala; cover design by
John Clark and Associates.*
Typesetting by Pardy's Printers, Ringwood, Hants.
*Printed in Great Britain by Jolly & Barber Ltd,
Rugby, Warwicks.*

British Library Cataloguing in Publication Data
Mackay, James A.
    Stamp collecting : philatelic terms
    illustrated.—3rd ed.—(Stanley
    Gibbons stamp collecting series)
    1. Postage-stamps—Collectors and
    collecting—Dictionaries
    I. Title
    769.56'03'21   HE6196

    ISBN 0-85259-157-8

S.G. Item No. 2740

PREFACE

Like all activities, philately has a language of its own. Collectors need to be conversant with this in order to understand their catalogues, handbooks and magazines. Many of the terms used relate to the physical characteristics of stamps—watermark, perforation, paper, etc.—others to the nature of a stamp design, others to the postmarks used to cancel stamps. In the past collectors have tended to ignore postal material other than postage stamps themselves. In more recent times the more enlightened collector has come to realise that the stamp is just part of the story—of equal interest and importance are the covers on which stamp travelled through the post, postal markings other than that used to cancel the stamp and the host of associated labels affixed to indicate the postal service used. Gradually the hobby of stamp collecting has come to include what is commonly—if erroneously—referred to as 'postal history'. Both 'stamp collecting' and 'postal history' come under the umbrella term 'philately'.

Guides to philatelic terms—or stamp dictionaries—are not new. Indeed the Philatelic Congress of Great Britain (now incorporated into the British Philatelic Federation) first published a *Glossary of Philatelic Terms* in 1912; further editions appeared in 1933 and 1951. For the most part these were confined to stamp terms and were unillustrated.

Stanley Gibbons were fortunate to acquire a collection of stamps and related material arranged according to philatelic terms and this unusual (perhaps unique) reference collection was displayed to many philatelic societies in Great Britain. This collection formed the basis of the original edition of *Philatelic Terms Illustrated*, first published as a part-work in Gibbons *Stamp Monthly* and subsequently in book form. The collection contained material to about 1950, and was supplemented by material in other S.G. reference collections.

Since the second edition of *PTI* was published in 1978 a number of new terms have come into use and interest in postal services has increased. Thus it was decided to give *PTI* a thorough overhaul so that a new edition would prove as comprehensive and as useful as its predecessors. We were pleased to enlist the help of James Mackay—a noted author and philatelic journalist and the doyen of British postal history studies with an impressive list of publications to his credit. Mr Mackay has carefully updated the text of Russell Bennett and James Watson, augmented it—particularly in respect to postal history—and made available for illustration many items from his extensive collection.

No glossary is ever likely to be 100 per cent complete but we hope that in this new edition collectors will find clearly defined the vast majority of terms they will come across in their reading. If it helps them understand philatelic literature and be better able to appreciate the material in their collections, it will have served its purpose well.

Stanley Gibbons Publications Ltd

USING THIS BOOK

The entries in this book are alphabetically arranged—this makes it both simple to use and avoids the need for an index. A few terms are also referred to by philatelists using an alternative term—in such cases a cross reference to the more commonplace terms will be found alongside the less frequently used term. For example the reader looking for a definition of the term *Acheson's Graphite* is referred to the entry under *Naphthadag*.

Many terms can only be defined by using other philatelic terms and it would be tedious for the reader if further definitions were given within a single entry. For example under the entry relating to the term *Albino*, the reader is referred to the terms *Embossed stamps, postal stationery, postmarks, overprints* and *surcharges*. These terms are printed in bold type so as to make them easily seen. The collector seeking further information is recommended to turn to those entries. Related terms are sometimes referred to, using the prefix *See also*. Such references have been kept to the minimum; as far as is possible each entry is self-contained.

ILLUSTRATIONS

Most terms have an accompanying illustration—mostly in black and white and captioned with the appropriate philatelic term. As a general rule stamps are illustrated 'actual size' with covers and other material reduced to a manageable size. Where terms are illustrated in colour, reference to the colour plates is shown at the end of the entry by the symbol ■.

COVER ILLUSTRATIONS

Front cover — Field Post Office cancel (Czech troops in UK, Second World War); Coin Daté (French 1957 definitive, date of printing 14.11.58); Se-tenant (German 10pf. and 15pf. stamps from booklet pane, 1918); Unusual perforations (Bussahir first issues had large holes, gauging between 7 and 11½); Flaw (Ukraine, blank corner caused by intervening paper); Deliberate Error (USA Dag Hammarskjöld stamp with inverted yellow, 1962).
Back cover — Balloon post (ballon monté cover, Siege of Paris, 1870); Pillars (horizontal pillars in interpanneau gutter, GB 4½d. 'Jubilee' issue.

THE AUTHOR

James Mackay began stamp collecting at the age of four, his first album being a copy of the prewar Highway Code in which his earliest specimens were stuck down with glue. He graduated to proper stamp-hinges and a printed album three years later. In 1961 he became the world's youngest philatelic curator, in charge of the collections in the British Museum. Since 1971 he has been a full-time author and journalist, contributing a regular column on philately and numismatics to the *Financial Times*. With over seventy titles to his credit, he has probably authored more books on philately and postal history than anyone else. He writes extensively in the philatelic press, including *Gibbons Stamp Monthly*.

Foremost among his other interests are languages and piano playing (with a preference for Bach and Scott Joplin). He also writes extensively on other collectibles and the applied and decorative arts.

PHILATELIC TERMS ILLUSTRATED

ABNORMAL. Term applied specifically to certain stamps produced by De La Rue for Great Britain, 1862–80, from plates which were not subsequently put into normal production. De La Rue submitted to the Board of Inland Revenue the first six sheets of stamps produced from each plate. These stamps were imperforate but gummed and watermarked. The Board retained one sheet as the Imprimatur and the other five sheets were either destroyed or perforated and put into circulation. Normally these five sheets would be the same as all others produced from the same plate, but sometimes plates were modified or scrapped, or a change was made in the colour used for the normal printing. The resultant stamps from the five sheets were therefore classified as Abnormals. Only 12 types of Abnormal have so far been recorded, although there are a further nine plates which were registered but from which no stamps are known to exist. ■

ACHESON'S GRAPHITE. *See* Naphthadag.

ACKNOWLEDGMENT OF RECEIPT. Popular though incorrect term for a postal service known as Advice of Delivery.

ADDITIONAL HALFPENNY TAX. A charge levied by the British Post Office on letters transmitted within, to or from Scotland if conveyed at any point of their journey by vehicles having more than two wheels. This tax was introduced in 1813 in a half-hearted attempt to raise money to pay the tolls levied by the turnpike trusts on mailcoaches which had previously been exempted from such charges. The net result of this impost, however, was to reduce the number of mailcoach services in Scotland. Many post offices in Scotland, and the larger offices in England and Ireland, employed distinctive handstamps to denote the charge which continued until the advent of Uniform Postage late in 1839.

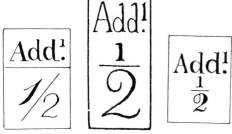

Scottish Additional Halfpenny Tax handstamps

ADHESIVE POSTAGE STAMPS. Stamps intended to be affixed to postal packets by means of gum or some other adhesive substance, as distinct from a handstruck stamp, a stamp impressed or embossed on postal stationery, a meter mark, postage paid impression or any other device denoting the prepayment of postage. The first adhesive postage stamps, the Great Britain 1d and 2d of 1840, arose from Rowland Hill's suggestion of "a bit of paper just large enough to bear the stamp and covered at the back with a glutinous wash which the user might, by applying a little moisture, attach to the back of the letter". This published proposal antedated by several months the similar suggestion of "stamped slips" made by James Chalmers of Dundee. *See also* Ungummed Stamps.

The Penny Black—World's first adhesive postage stamp

ADSONS. Nickname given to postage stamps of the 1893 series, issued by New Zealand with commercial advertising on their backs. A different advertisement appeared on the back of each stamp so that it is possible to reconstruct whole sheets on the basis of these advertisements, which included Beecham's pills, Sunlight soap, Fry's cocoa and Cadbury's chocolate. It should be noted that British stamps are known with PEARS SOAP printed on their backs, an unofficial experiment of 1887.

ADVERTISEMENT ON POSTMARKS. The use of postmarks to draw the attention of the public to goods and services goes back to 1661 when a handstamp was applied to letters in London destined for addresses along the Kent road. The nine-line text in a circular frame announced that "The Post for all Kent goes every night from the Round House in Love Lane & comes every morning." A similar mark advertised the Essex post. These marks were short-lived and advertising, by means of slogan postmarks, was not adopted till the late-19th century. Commercial advertising, though officially banned in Britain, has appeared indirectly in certain slogans giving company names or logotypes. Both France and Italy have sanctioned commercial advertising in postmarks. Otherwise postmark advertisements have been confined to tourist and industrial publicity and announcements of a national or international nature.

Advertisements on Postmarks

ADVERTISEMENTS ON STAMPS. Commercial advertising appeared on the Mulready envelopes and wrappers of 1840–1, this version being sold by advertising companies at a discount. Between 1857 and 1893 the Post Office permitted companies to have advertising rings round the embossed stamps on their postal stationery, but only nine firms availed themselves of this. The earliest adhesive stamps to incorporate commercial advertising were American local stamps issued in 1862 by the California City Letter Express Co. Since 1911

many countries have permitted advertising on the coupons attached to stamps sold in booklets or coils. Advertising on the back of stamps was revived in 1964 when Sierra Leone pioneered self-adhesive stamps with advertising matter on the backing paper. Advertisements may also be found in the selvage of sheets and booklet panes. Apart from the Mulready wrappers, advertising on postal stationery appears to have been confined to New Zealand and the local posts of Germany. *See also* Publicity Stamps.

Italian stamp advertising Campari

ADVERTISING LABELS. Adhesive labels bearing the name, logotype and/or slogan of a commercial company, widely used as an advertising medium on firms' mail before the advent of metered mail. The earliest example recorded is a circular label of the Apollo candle factory of Vienna, issued in 1845 for the National Trade and Industry Exhibition, but half a century elapsed before such labels, often associated with exhibitions, became popular. They attained their peak in the early years of this century, but were largely superseded by postage meters which offered a more effective form of advertising. Nevertheless they continued to be produced, often in connection with exhibitions or celebrating firms' anniversaries, and appear to have gained in popularity in recent years.

Advertising labels—Stanley Gibbons/Harrison & Sons (1957)

ADVICE OF DELIVERY. An international service, ratified by the Universal Postal Union in 1890 and adopted by member countries in March 1891, permitting the sender of a registered packet, on payment of a fee, to be notified of the delivery of the packet. The service is known in French as *Avis de Reception* and denoted by the letters "AR" found on postmarks, postal stationery and labels. A few countries even issued special stamps for this purpose. Colombia issued stamps in 1865 inscribed "A" (Anotacion) or "R" (Rejistro) denoting registration and acknowledgment of receipt respectively. Stamps inscribed "AR" (Aviso de Recepcion) were issued from 1894 till 1917. Stamps for this service were also issued by Chile (1894), El Salvador (1897) and Montenegro (1895–1913).

Advice of Delivery

AEROGRAMMES. Lightweight postal stationery, otherwise known as Air Letter Sheets, used for the economical transmission of letters by air. The first air letter sheets were issued by Colombia (SCADTA) and Germany in 1923. Lightweight stationery inscribed "Air-o-Gram" was devised by RB Jackson and used in Thailand in 1932–3. None of these sheets had franking validity and therefore required adhesive stamps to be affixed. In July 1933 Iraq issued stamped air letter sheets devised by Douglas Gumley. This form of stationery known then as an Air Mail Letter Card was the forerunner of the British sheets introduced in 1941 for mail to prisoners of war.

Aerogrammes for general use were adopted in June 1943 and have since spread throughout the world. Commemorative aerogrammes were issued from 1948 (Olympic Games) onwards, notably in Scotland where two issues have appeared annually in recent years.

AFFIXING MACHINES. Mechanical devices, either manually operated or worked by electricity, used to save time and labour in affixing stamps to firms' correspondence. The earliest machine of this type was marketed in 1907 by the Detroit Mailing Machine Company. In connexion with affixing machines some postal administrations (e.g. USA and New Zealand) produced imperforate coils which were then privately perforated by the manufacturers. In Britain stamps for use in such machines were produced in side-delivery coils (as opposed to front-delivery coils used in vending machines), hence the sideways watermark found in such stamps. The use of these machines has largely been superseded by the use of metered mail and postage paid impressions.

AIRGRAPH. Special letter form used by British forces during the Second World War. Letters were written on special forms which were then microfilmed. The microfilm was flown to England, processed by Kodak at Wealdstone, Harrow and the prints put into special window envelopes for transmission through the normal inland post to their destination. Between 21 April 1941 and 31 July 1945 some 350 million airgraphs were transmitted. This service, in fact, was inspired by a system of microfilming messages used during the Siege of Paris in 1870–1. *See also* Siege Posts and V Mail.

*Aerogrammes—plain
and pictorial*

Second World War Airgraph

AIR LETTER SHEET. *See* Aerogramme.

AIRMAIL. Any form of correspondence transmitted by air. It thus encompasses everything from **Pigeon Post** and **Balloon Post** to **Helicopter, Parachute** and **Rocket Mail**, as well as the carriage of postal packets and parcels by conventional aircraft. The first official carriage of mail by air took place in August 1859 between La Fayette and Crawfordsville, Indiana by the balloon Jupiter, authorised by the local postmaster. The first government-operated airmail took place from Metz and to and from Paris during the Franco-German War of 1870–1. Mail was carried unofficially by heavier-than-air machine in 1908 (Paris-St Nazaire), but the first official airmail by this means was the Allahabad-Naini service, India in February 1911. Britain, Denmark, Italy and the USA all operated official services later that year. *See also* Catapult Mail, First Flight Cover, Glider Mail and Propaganda Leaflets.

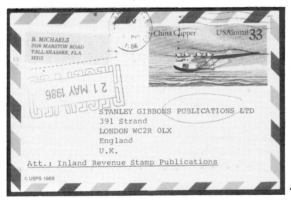

Airmail

AIRMAIL LABELS. Otherwise known as Etiquettes, these labels are used to mark packets for air transmission in a highly distinctive manner. They were first used in February 1912 (inscribed FLUGPOST) for the Bork-Bruck flight by Grade. The words PAR AVION ("by bird") first appeared in a handstruck **cachet** in 1913 and in French labels from 1918. The UPU decreed that airmail labels should be thus inscribed, along with the language of the issuing country. Britain, Denmark, the Netherlands and Sweden all began using such labels in 1920. Although blue is the predominant colour, variety is imparted by the use of national and airline emblems and inscriptions in a second colour.

AIRMAIL LABELS USED AS POSTAGE STAMPS. Airmail labels were issued by the Portuguese colony of Mozambique in 1932 with a space for the insertion of the air fee in manuscript. In 1937 the air fee was combined with the postal charge, denoted by the inscriptions, in French and Portuguese, signifying "Charge Paid". These labels were cancelled in the same manner as postage stamps.

AIRMAIL STAMPS. Postage stamps denoting the prepayment of fees for transmission by air. The earliest was a 5c issued in 1877 by Samuel King for mail carried by his balloon Buffalo from Nashville, Tennessee. In 1898 stamps were produced for the Original Great Barrier Pigeongram Service and many other private issues appeared in 1909–14 for aviation meetings and pioneer flights. The first official air stamp was a 25c issued by Italy in May 1917. Since 1918 most countries have issued airmail stamps although the only British ones have the status of **private** or **semi-official**. It is worth noting, however, that many definitives, and the majority of commemoratives since 1953, have been issued primarily for airmail usage.

Airmail stamps

Airmail Labels (Etiquettes)

AIRSTREAM. A service of the British Post Office, introduced in 1986, for the bulk posting of airmail packets using **postage paid impressions** and a distinctive label.

AIRWAY LETTER STAMPS. Stamps issued by British European Airways (later British Airways) since 1951, and also for a while by Cambrian Airways, for the carriage of letters between airports and for posting on arrival. Such stamps therefore perform a service similar to that provided by railway letter stamps.

ALBINO. Deficient pigmentation in animals resulting in a white, colourless appearance. The term is used philatelically to denote a lack of colour, due to the omission of ink during printing or by the interpolation of foreign matter on the printing cylinder or plate. **Embossed stamps** or **postal stationery** were especially prone to this, but it may also be found in **postmarks**, **overprints** and **surcharges**.

Airway Letter Stamp

ALL-OVER WATERMARK. A single device or pattern embracing the entire sheet of stamps. In such cases a certain proportion of the stamps may show no trace of watermark at all. *See also* Sheet Watermark.

All-over Watermark—Rumanian coat of arms

ALPHABET LETTERS. The **check letters** on the line-engraved issues of Great Britain, 1840–80 are classified into four alphabets, according to the characteristics of the letters punched into the printing plates during manufacture and are thus a useful feature in assigning individual stamps to the correct plate.

Alphabet Letters

ANAGLYPH. Printing in two colours to create a three-dimensional effect. An image superimposed on a similar image slightly out of alignment creates this allusion when viewed through filters or '3–D spectacles'. The 25 and 60 lire stamps marking Italy's entry into the UN, 1956 are so far the only philatelic examples of this technique. ■

ANAGLYPTOGRAPHY. Engraving process which conveys the impression of relief to a print by means of parallel wavy lines. Prime examples of the technique are the effigies on Austria's 1 and 2g stamps (1890) and the George V series of Australia (1913–21).

Anaglyptography—Francis Joseph of Austria

ANHYPHENATE. Without a hyphen, and thus distinguishing the early stamps of South Africa inscribed SUIDAFRIKA instead of SUID-AFRIKA, and in particular the GB 6d of 1869 which differed from the issues of 1865–7 by omitting the hyphen between SIX and PENCE.

Anhyphenate

ANILINE COLOUR. Strictly speaking, any colour with a coal-tar base, but used philatelically to denote aqueous (water-soluble) fugitive inks with a dye base that runs when wetted and fluoresces strongly under the **quartz lamp**. Stamps of this type exhibit a peculiar quality of brightness coupled with a suffusion of colour on the surface and the colour showing through to a marked degree on the back. ■

ARC ROULETTE. Form of separation, also known by the French term *percé en arc*, in which curved cuts appear as scalloped edges on the stamps.

Arc Roulette (Brunswick)

ARCHER ROULETTE AND PERFORATION. Experimental methods of separating stamps devised by Henry Archer. The first experiment, in 1848, produced stamps rouletted 12, but later Archer invented a machine which punched out and removed tiny discs of paper. After prolonged negotations, culminating in a Parliamentary enquiry, Archer was awarded £4000 for his rights in 1853 and from 1854 onwards all British adhesive stamps, with the exception of the embossed 6d, the **automatic stamps** and **self-adhesive stamps** used in **Post-a-Book** and **premium offers** have been perforated.

Archer Roulette (GB Penny Red)

ARMY POST. Special stamps thus inscribed were issued by Egypt from 1936 to 1951 for use by British forces stationed in the Canal Zone for the prepayment of the **concessionary postage** on their mail to the UK.

Army Post stamp (Egypt)

ARROW BLOCK. A block of stamps bearing in the attached selvage an arrow to indicate convenient points for folding or dividing the sheet.

Arrow Block

AUTHORISED DELIVERY STAMPS. Stamps inscribed RECAPITO AUTORIZZATO and issued by Italy since 1928 to denote the tax levied on certain classes of mail permitted to be delivered by private services. For this reason these stamps have been largely ignored (outside Italy) as either **fiscal stamps** or of no postal validity. Nevertheless, they are an official issue of the Italian Post Office and are fully listed in Italian catalogues.

Authorised Delivery Stamp (Italy)

AUTHORISED NON-PROFIT ORGANISATION STAMPS. Stamps issued by the US Post Office to prepay special concessionary rates of postage on the correspondence of charities and other institutions. Such stamps may be recognised by their odd amounts - e.g. 3.1c, 3.5c (1979–80), 5.2c and 5.9c (1982–3) as well as the tiny inscription alongside. In addition to these adhesive stamps, special postal stationery has also been issued. *See also* Bulk Rate Stamps.

Authorised Non-Profit Organisation Stamp (USA)

Automatic Letter Facing— machine cancellation

AUTOMATIC LETTER FACING (ALF). System invented by the British Post Office for the mechanisation of mail and first adopted at Southampton in 1957. ALF machines electronically scan mail at the primary sorting stage, first arranging the items so that they are 'faced' (i.e. the right way up, with the stamps in the upper right-hand position), then segregating items into first and second class mail. In connection with the early experiments stamps had graphite lines printed on their backs, but later phosphor bands were applied across their face. Apart from the graphite and phosphor variants in postage stamps, collectors distinguish the ALF dies in cancelling machines, usually characterised by alphanumeric codes. Nowadays the Post Office prefers the terms ASM (Automatic Sorting Machine) and FCT (Facer Cancelling Table) to denote the equipment used.

AUTOMATIC MACHINE PERFORATION. Distinctive types of perforation applied to the vertical spaces between stamps of New Zealand (1905–6) and the USA (1906–12). These stamps were supplied in imperforate coils for use in automatic dispensing and **affixing machines**, and the manufacturers then arranged to have the stamps perforated between in order to facilitate separation. These perforations include oblong slots, large round holes, **hyphen perforation** and various forms of **roulette**.

Automatic Machine Perforation (New Zealand, USA)

AUTOMATIC STAMPS. Also known by the German term *Automatenmarken* (ATM), they may be described as any impression applied directly to a postal packet or to a gummed label for affixing to a postal packet, dispensed by a coin-operated machine. Such machines may have a fixed value, a limited range of values or an infinite variety of denominations up to a certain limit. The earliest patent for such a machine was taken out by Carl Bushe in 1884 but it was not until 1900 that Christian Kahrs invented a coin-operated machine which was given a trial in Oslo. The insertion of 5 or 1O ore coins produced green or red impressions denoting the inland postcard and letter rates. A second machine with a more elaborate impression was tested in 1903–5. Trials with similar machines by Hollinsworth, Husband and Moss took place in Brisbane, Melbourne and Christchurch in 1903 but only New Zealand persevered and continued to use such machines, installed outside major post offices, until recently. These machines applied the impression direct to the postcard or letter. A trial with a machine by Ernest Wilkinson took place in London in 1912. The use of automatic stamps was largely superseded by the advent of **metered mail** from 1922 onwards, but this system was adapted by the US Post Office, following trials by Pitney-Bowes at Stamford, Conn in 1936–7. Known as **Mailomat**, it

was introduced in May 1939 at major post offices. These coin-operated machines give a gummed label resembling a meter mark but distinguished by the letters P and O at the sides of the date. These machines are now installed in department stores and railway stations as well as the lobbies of post offices. Also classed as automatic stamps are the **parcel stamps** dispensed by TIM, Setright and other machines used by the British Post Office (1947–69) and the Irish Post Office to this day. In August 1976 Switzerland introduced machines by the FRAMA Company at four offices. These machines are coin-operated and dispense gummed labels whose denomination is determined by pressing buttons. **Frama Labels** are now used in many countries, although they were short-lived (1984–5) in Great Britain. Automatic stamps also include the Postal Charges Calculator labels introduced in Australia in 1984. These are dispensed from machines which calculate the weight, postage and other fees due on postal packets and even produce a receipt for the sender. Similar machines are also used in Singapore and South Africa.

Automatic Stamps—(GB and Norway)

BACKPRINTING. *See* Printed on Back.

BACKSTAMP. Postmark applied to the backs of envelopes, wrappers and other postal packets. From 1840 the datestamp of the office of posting was applied as a backstamp, while the **Maltese Cross** and later the numbered obliterator were used to cancel the stamp. The datestamps of transit offices and the office of delivery were also applied as backstamps. Outward backstamping ceased when the **duplex cancellation** was adopted in the 1850s. Inward backstamping of inland letters was waived during the Christmas period in the early 1900s and gradually died out in 1906–10. Inward backstamping of overseas mail survived till the 1920s, but since then only registered packets have been backstamped, and even this practice has declined very considerably in recent years.

BALLOON POST. Mail carried by manned or unmanned free balloon. Although occasional letters were carried by, or dropped from, balloons from the 1780s onwards, the first attempt to operate an official balloon post came in 1859, between La Fayette and Crawfordsville, Indiana by the balloon Jupiter. During the siege of Metz, 1870, letters were flown by unmanned balloons, known as the "Papillons de Metz". Later mail was carried by manned balloon (*par Ballon monté*) or unmanned balloon (*par Ballon non monté*) from Paris during the siege of 1870–1. Souvenir mail was carried by balloon at many fairs and exhibitions in Europe at the turn of the century, and from 1909 to 1939 mail was carried by dirigible balloons in and from Germany (*see* Zeppelin Posts). Mail was flown by balloon during the siege of Przemysl in 1914–15 but in more recent years philatelic mail has been flown by demonstration balloons and also in connection with balloon races.

Backstamp—Ringwood (point of despatch), Dar-es-Salaam (arrival)

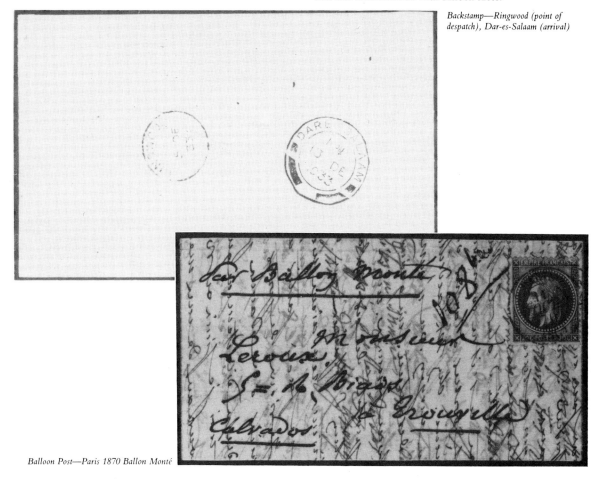

Balloon Post—Paris 1870 Ballon Monté

Banknote Paper—Latvia, 1919–20

BANDELETTE. Alternative name for Dominical Label.

BANKNOTE PAPER. Paper used originally in the production of banknotes, but subsequently employed for the printing of stamps. In 1920 Latvia issued Red Cross stamps which were printed on sheets of unfinished banknotes, both Bolshevist and White Russian (Bermondt-Avaloff) notes being used. These stamps show portions of banknotes on their back. An experimental printing of British 1d stamps was made on banknote paper; they were never issued but exist imperforate with a CANCELLED overprint.

BANTAMS. Nickname given to stamps of South Africa, 1942–4, printed in a reduced format in order to save paper.

Bantams—South Africa, 1942–4

BAR CANCEL. Cancellation consisting of bars, in rectangular, oval or circular patterns. Such cancellations, incorporating numerals with or without letters, were widely used in the 19th century. Mute cancellations of this type were used to denote stamps of North Borneo **cancelled to order**.

Bar Cancels on Victorian stamps

BAR-CODE STAMPS AND LABELS. Bar-codes are patterns of straight lines of varying thickness which are capable of being read by electronic equipment, and are a familiar sight on everything from paper-backs to packaged goods. A bar-code forms an integral part of the distinctive label used by the British Post Office in its **Trakback** service, introduced in 1986. Japan now uses self-adhesive **registration labels** on which the serial numbers are bar-coded.

Bar-Code registration label (Japan)

BARRED. Description applied to **bar cancels** but also denoting stamps which have been overprinted with bars to blot out the effigy of an overthrown ruler, e.g. the 1953 issues of Egypt (portrait of ex-king Farouk), Hitler Head stamps of Germany, 1945–6, Iran 1979 (portrait of the Shah). Overprints of parallel bars were also applied to certain American and Canadian stamps intended for use as **pre-cancels**.

BÂTONNÉ. French word meaning "ruled", used to describe paper having a watermark of parallel lines about a centimetre apart, originally as a guide to handwriting. The basic paper may be either 'wove' (plain) or 'laid' (with closely-set parallel lines), known as 'wove bâtonné' or 'laid bâtonné'.

Barred—cancel (N. Borneo), obliteration of overthrown ruler (Egypt), telegraphic use (Spain)

Batonne paper—Poonch, India (1877–84)

BICYCLE POSTS. Postal services operated by means of bicycles have included the Coolgardie Cycle Express (1893), the Fresno and San Francisco Bicycle Mail (1894), the Lake Lefroy Goldfield Cycle Mail (1897), the Italian Coralit service (1944) and the Moulins service at Timaru, New Zealand (1968). Special stamps were issued in each case.

Bicycle Posts

BILINGUAL PAIRS. Two unseparated stamps on which the inscriptions are in different languages. Bilingual pairs were issued by South Africa from 1926 to 1951, stamps being inscribed alternately in English and Afrikaans. Other countries to have issued stamps in bilingual pairs have included South West Africa, Belgium (French and Flemish) and Sri Lanka (Tamil and Sinhala).

Bilingual Pair (South Africa/Suid Afrika)

BIPARTITE STAMPS AND LABELS. Stamps and labels printed in two parts for easy separation, so that one part can be affixed to a packet and the other retained as a receipt of posting. Bipartite stamps were issued by the Drammen local post (1868) and the Kotelnich Zemstvo post (1869). The latter, in fact, ranks as the world's rarest stamp, as only the counterfoil half of

one stamp is known to exist, the portion affixed to the letter having disappeared. The appearance of the complete stamp is known, as it was illustrated in the Moens catalogue of 1880! Bipartite stamps were issued by Italy 1914–54 for parcel post, the left-hand portion being affixed to the parcel card and the right-hand portion to the sender's receipt. Bipartite postage due labels have been issued by Rumania since 1947, the right-hand portion being affixed to the surcharged packet and the left-hand portion being kept by the delivery postman as a receipt.

Bipartite Stamps (Italy, Rumania)

BISECT. Half of a stamp which has been cut or perforated in two to furnish an authorised denomination of half the original face value, or otherwise surcharged. Bisects are commonly found with horizontal or diagonal cuts, occasionally with vertical divisions. They were mostly cut with knives or scissors, but those issued in Portuguese India, Lourenzo Marques and Argentina were specially surcharged and perforated.

BISHOP MARK. The earliest dated postmark known to have been used by any postal administration, it consisted of a small circle divided in two with the day and month indicated in respective segments. It takes its name from Colonel Sir Henry Bishop, Postmaster General in 1660–3. Announcing the adoption of this mark on 2 August 1661, Bishop wrote "A stamp is invented that is putt upon every letter showing the date of the moneth that every letter comes to this office..". Bishop marks were used in London from 1661 to 1787, but spread to Dublin (1670–1795), Edinburgh (1693–1806), Albany (1773–87), Boston (1768–1800), Charlestown (1768–75), New York (1758–76), Quebec (1776–99), Philadelphia (1766–76) and Calcutta (1775–7). Modified forms of the Bishop mark, using large initial letters with the day and month, were used at Bristol and Exeter from 1697 on Cross-Post letters.

Bisects (Portuguese India)

Bishop Mark

Bizonals (Germany 1945–9)   *Black Bar (Early GB phosphor issues)*

BIZONALS. Nickname given to stamps issued from 1945 to 1949 in the Anglo-American zones of occupied Germany.

BLACK BAR. Marginal marking printed alongside the arrows on certain sheets of British stamps with **phosphor bands** to assist checking in the PO Supplies Department.

Black Print (Austrian stamps)

BLACK PRINT. Proofs printed in black and affixed by the Austrian postal administration to press notices announcing each new issue. The term has also been used rather loosely in recent years to describe other philatelic items, such as monochrome prints of British stamps prepared as souvenirs of philatelic exhibitions or as giveaway material with certain magazines.

BLACKOUT CANCEL. Form of mute cancellation adopted in Canada during the Second World War, the name being removed from machine dater dies for security reasons and replaced by a solid black arc. A similar device, however, was also used in a demonstration cancelling die used at the Post Office pavilion in the Glasgow Empire Exhibition, 1938.

Blackout Cancel (Glasgow exhibition, war security)

BLEED-OFF. Printing term denoting printing which runs off the edge of a page after trimming. It has also been applied to stamps whose printing runs off into the perforations instead of terminating in a colourless border. This technique was pioneered by Egypt, many of whose stamps since 1946 had the design running off into the perforations. It has been extensively used by other countries in recent years.

BLEUTÉ. *See* Blued Paper.

BLIND PERFORATION. Term applied to perforation where the holes are not punched out, due to blunt or missing perforating pins which leave the paper depressed or unmarked.

BLITZ PERFORATIONS. Perforations applied in 1940–1 by Waterlow and Sons to stamps of the New Zealand series of 1936–43. De La Rue, who normally produced these stamps, were temporarily out of action because of the Blitzkrieg air-raids on London, and the stamps had to be perforated by Waterlows, who used a different gauge.

BLOCK OF STAMPS. Any multiple of unsevered stamps, other than a complete pane or sheet, which contains at least two parallel rows of stamps in any direction.

Blind Perforation (Samoa, USA)

Bleed-off

Block of Stamps (fine used from Italy)

BLOCKED VALUE. Name given to one denomination in each set of stamps issued by the German Democratic Republic between 1955 and 1982, the sale of which was severely restricted. This practice effectively controlled the philatelic traffic in these stamps and was designed to prevent speculation and the use of stamps to circumvent currency regulations. A glance at the stamp catalogue will show which stamps were the blocked values, as their philatelic value usually far exceeds that of other denominations.

BLUE SAFETY PAPER. Paper containing prussiate of potash, added during manufacture, to prevent the printing ink penetrating deeply into the paper. Any attempt to remove the postmark by chemical means would therefore remove the design as well. The prussiate produced a blue appearance in the inked areas of the British stamps of 1841–56, due to chemical reaction. *See also* Ivory Head. ■

BLUED PAPER. Paper with a pale blue tinge, caused by chemicals in the paper or printing ink, or by a reaction of one with the other. Blued paper was used for many British postage and fiscal stamps printed by De La Rue using the letterpress process up to 1884. ■

BOGUS STAMP. A stamp which is fictitious. These stamps may be produced for fictitious countries or non-existent postal services; or they may be produced ostensibly for real places but used primarily for political propaganda purposes (e.g. the stamps of the South Moluccas or Nagaland); or they may be produced purely for the philatelic market. Samuel Allan Taylor of Boston specialised in the production of bogus stamps, including the notorious Fenian stamps which had the unique distinction of being reproduced on two Irish stamps of 1967.

Bogus Stamps—Nagaland (India), Thomond (Ireland), Albania, Croatia

Booklet (GB 50p, issued 1979)

BOOKLET. Small panes of stamps bound together in card covers, often with sheets of interleaving bearing commercial advertising. They were pioneered by Luxembourg in 1895 and first issued by Britain in 1904. Booklets are often made up from sheets specially printed for this purpose, with a narrow **selvage** at one side of each pane for binding. Guillotining of individual booklets frequently results in the perforations on the outer edges of panes being trimmed off. Odd amounts in booklet panes are often balanced by the use of se-tenant **coupons** which themselves may be used to carry advertisements. The earliest British booklets were sold for a halfpenny extra to cover to cost of production; nowadays the customer benefits from booklets containing 51p worth of stamps, by inserting a 50p coin in a slot machine. Stamps from such **discount** booklets can be recognised by the blue star printed on the back. Another British innovation was the sponsored booklet (1959) which developed a decade later into the **prestige booklet**. Since 1968 many British booklets have had pictorial covers issued in thematic sets, a practice which has since extended to many other countries.

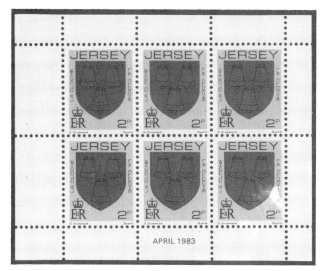

Booklet Pane (Jersey, 1983)

Booklet Stamps (Isle of Man, 1979–80)

Brunswick Star (Edinburgh postmark, 1863–71)

BOOKLET PANE. Pair, strip or block of stamps intended for issue in booklets and distinguishable from stamps issued in normal sheets by (a) being imperforate on the outer edges, (b) incorporating coupons bearing advertisements, a **St Andrew's Cross** or some other device, (c) different denominations printed se-tenant, or (d) some form of security backprint.

BOOKLET STAMPS. Stamps intended for release in booklets and differing in some respect from stamps issued in normal sheets, as detailed above. In some cases, however, special stamps, only available in booklets, are used.

BOULE DE MOULINS. Zinc-coated steel spheres containing bundles of letters wrapped in waterproof material, which were floated down the River Seine into Paris during the siege of 1870-1. Many of these Boules were sunk by German gunfire but over the ensuing century they were occasionally dredged up from the river bed, their contents dried out and attempts made to deliver the letters. The most recent recovery occurred at Rouen in 1968. A Boule was depicted on one of the French Europa stamps of 1979. ∎

BROKEN LETTERS. Malformed or broken letters in the inscriptions on stamps caused by damage to, or deterioration in, the printing plate, cylinder or type.

BRUNSWICK STAR. Experimental postmark used at Edinburgh, 1863–71 in connexion with trials of the Pearson Hill Pivot and Parallel Motion stamp-cancelling machines. At least 20 types were used in that period, most of them being very short-lived, and consequently this series of postmarks is scarce and much sought after. The series takes its name from the radiate breast-star in the Hanoverian Order of Brunswick which it was thought the earlier designs resembled.

Broken Letters (GB 'F' for 'E' in 'PENCE', etc.)

BULK POSTING. Since the 1850s facilities have been provided by the British Post Office for the cash prepayment of packets posted in bulk. From 1870 cheaper rates of postage were allowed in respect of printed matter, but since the mid-1960s discounts and cheaper rates have been available through the Rebate and Deferred Posting schemes, provided that packets (including postcards) are of a uniform size and weight and agreed minimum postings are made on each occasion. Such postings were originally denoted by red machine "Paid" postmarks incorporating the letters "R" (Rebate), "BP" (Bulk Posting) or "DP" (Deferred Posting), the lastnamed indicating bulk mail which was delivered at the convenience of the Post Office and therefore subject to delay. Since 1966 bulk posting has increasingly been denoted by PPIs or Postage Paid Impressions incorporating numerals "1" or "2" (first or second-class mail), "P" (parcels) or "R" (rebate posting). Similar systems exist in many other countries. In the USA, Canada and New Zealand, for example, a system of **permit mailing** has been in operation for many years.

Bulk Posting—Rebate Mail postmark

BULK RATE STAMPS. Special low-denomination adhesive stamps for use on bulk-posted mail. Between 1922 and 1954 the USA issued half-cent stamps specifically for this purpose, and since then many other stamps with fractional denominations have been produced. Between 1975 and 1985 these stamps were actually inscribed to denote Bulk Posting or use by Authorised Non-Profit Organisations, but since then these and other specific usages have been indicated in the overprint applied as a **pre-cancel**. Bulk Rate stamps have also been issued by France, similarly recognisable by odd amounts and pre-cancellation.

Bulk Rate Stamps (USA, 1976)

BUREAU PRINTS. Term applied generally to stamps produced by the Bureau of Engraving and Printing, Washington, but more specifically applied to a form of pre-cancellation overprinted on stamps issued from the Bureau, as distinct from the **pre-cancels** applied locally.

BURÉLAGE. A fine pattern or network of lines or dots printed either on the face of a stamp but underneath the main design, or on the back of the stamp, as a security device. Prime examples of burelage on the face include the earliest stamps of Denmark while burelage on the back may be found on Queensland halfpenny stamps of the 1895–6 series. ∎

Burelage

BUS PARCEL STAMPS. Private stamps issued by bus companies to prepay freight charges on packets and parcels conveyed over their bus routes. These stamps, issued in many countries since the early 1900s, are an important aspect of local stamps. Bus Parcel stamps, however, have also been issued by the Finnish postal adminstration since 1949 in connection with parcels conveyed by motorcoach services. They may be recognised by their inscriptions AUTOPAKETTI and BUSSPAKET in Finnish and Swedish respectively.

Bus Parcel Stamps—Autopaketti (Finland) and English and Scottish bus company issues

Bypost Stamps— Bergen and Trondhjem

BYPOST STAMPS. Stamps issued by the municipal postal services which operated in many towns of Denmark and Norway in the 19th century, and deriving their name from the inscription BYPOST (literally "town post"). Stamps of this type were issued by Aalborg, Aarhus, Copenhagen, Fredericia, Holte, Holback, Horsens, Kolding, Odense, Randers, Svendborg, Veile and Viborg (Denmark) and Aalesund, Arendal, Bergen, Christansund, Drammen, Grimstad, Hammerfest, Holmestrand, Hortens, Levanger, Mandal, Namsos, Stenkjaer, Trondhjem, Tonsberg and Tromso (Norway).

CACHET. A printed, embossed or (usually) handstruck inscription or device impressed on a postal packet to denote the special circumstances in which it has been posted (e.g. an expedition, special flight or exhibition), or to indicate the class of postage or some form of special handling (e.g. Express). The cachet may be official and applied by the Post Office, or private or semi-official, and applied independently of the postal authority. *See also* Certifying Stamp.

Cachet—applied at Charity Fair, Dover 1963

CALENDERING. The technique by which paper is smoothed, using chilled steel rollers at the end of the manufacturing process.

CAMPAIGN COVER. Envelope, wrapper or other postal packet posted by military or naval personnel on active service in wartime, distinguished by endorsements such as "On Active Service – no stamps available", **cachets** of military units, **censor markings** or military postmarks.

Campaign Cover

CANCELLATION. A mark of defacement of any kind applied to a stamp or item of postal stationery to prevent it being used again. It may take the form of manuscript marking, machine or handstruck obliteration, piercing or punching with holes, or even the removal of a portion of the stamp, as in the case of the earliest stamps of Afghanistan. *See also* Obliteration, Postmark.

CANCELLED. Security endorsement, either overprinted or handwritten, to prevent stamps being used postally. It is known as a form of **Specimen** overprint on British and colonial stamps, and also overprinted in English or its equivalent in other languages, to denote remaindered stamps.

Cancelled stamps of GB and Mauritius

CANCELLED TO ORDER. Stamps which have been cancelled without actually performing postal service. Such stamps may have been remaindered, or they may have been removed from stock for sale to collectors at reduced rates. The term "Postmarked to Order" is sometimes used to distinguish stamps specially cancelled by favour at a Post Office counter, but which have been sold at full face value.

Cancelled To Order—modern Czechoslovak and Polish issues

CAPPED NUMERALS. Flaws resembling caps surmounting the figures "2" of the United States 2c Washington definitive of 1890–3.

Capped Numerals—US 2c. with capped '2'

CARDBOARD. Fine-quality card of varying degrees of thickness, used for proofing impressions of stamp dies and plates, and also in the manufacture of postcards, letter cards and certain other classes of postal stationery. Stamps of Russia and the Ukraine were also printed on cardboard with inscriptions on the back signifying their legal tender status as substitutes for subsidiary coinage during and immediately after the First World War. ∎

CARLIST STAMPS. Stamps authorised by Don Carlos and issued in certain Spanish provinces in 1873–4 when he assumed the title of King Carlos VII of Spain.

Carlist stamps (Carlos VII of Spain, 1873–4)

CARRIERS' STAMPS. Strictly speaking, stamps issued by carriers and freight companies to prepay the charges on packets conveyed by them. Specifically, however, the term is used to denote the stamps issued by carrier companies in the United States to indicate the charges on packets conveyed to or from local post offices prior to 1863 when general town delivery services were instituted. Some of these stamps were official issues of the USPO (e.g. the New York City Despatch and the Philadelphia PO stamps), while others were issued by private firms but with the sanction of the USPO. The first of these issues appeared in 1842 and ranked second only to the British stamps of 1840.

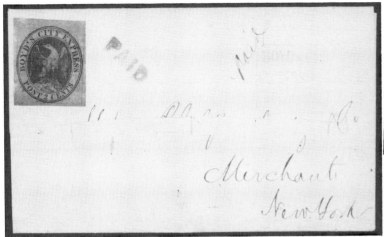

Carriers' Stamps

CARTRIDGE PAPER. Stout, hard, rough paper originally used in the manufacture of ammunition for small arms, but nowadays used mainly for drawing. It has occasionally been used for postage stamps, notably Trinidad's 1d blue of 1853 and Russia's Volga Famine charity set of 1921. ■

CASH ON DELIVERY LABELS. Labels issued by many post offices on packets on which trade charges (i.e. for the goods contained therein) are to be recovered from the addressee. Such a scheme was included in Professor Fawcett's plan for the British parcel post of 1883, but it was rejected by the Treasury, and it was left to countries in Europe to develop the COD system at the beginning of this century. Britain did not adopt the service till 1920, and then only in respect of parcels to certain colonies. The COD system was not extended to the inland mails until 29 March 1926. A distinctive feature of COD labels is that they are either triangular in shape, or have a prominent triangular motif as part of their design. Furthermore the triangle is usually printed in bright red or orange. Apart from the letters COD found on the British inland series, COD labels may be recognised by inscriptions such as "Remboursement" (French), "Reembolso" (Spanish), "Nachnahme" (German), "Dobirka" (Czech), "Rimborso" or "Assegno" (Italian) or "Postforskott" (Swedish). The Swiss labels are of particular interest as they incorporate the name of the office of issue.

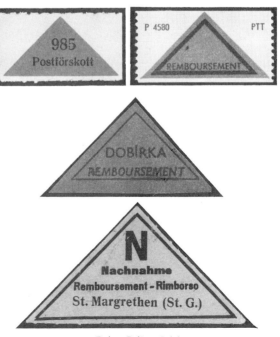

Cash on Delivery Labels

Catapult Mail—Catapulted from SS Bremen, 1929

Cavallini (Italian 'little horsemen')

Censor Marks and Labels (Second World War)

CATAPULT MAIL. Mail accelerated by a "ship to shore" service, involving the use of light aircraft catapulted from the decks of ships when within range of the shore. This service was pioneered by France in 1928 to accelerate trans-Atlantic mail carried by the liner *Ile de France*. Stamps portraying Pasteur and Berthelot were surcharged 10 francs (S.G. 464–5) in connexion with this service. Germany adopted a similar service in 1929, using the liners *Bremen* and *Europa* and mail transported by this means is known with distinctive **cachets**.

CAVALLINI. Italian for "little horsemen" and signifying the stamps impressed on letter sheets used in the kingdom of Sardinia from 1818 onwards. All letter sheets required to be stamped with impressions representing a tax, but as taxed letters were transmitted through the post at no additional cost these stamps may be regarded as postal rather than as **fiscal**.

CENSOR MARKS AND LABELS. Although censorship of correspondence has been practised by many governments for centuries, it is only within the past 250 years that marks and labels have been used quite openly to indicate that this has taken place. The earliest example known consists of manuscript endorsement "Open'd by Rebells" applied to letters detained by the Jacobites during the Rebellion of 1745–6. Censorship denoted by handstruck markings was practised during the Boer War (1899–1902), while the use of special labels to reseal packets opened for examination dates from the First World War. Mail liable to censorship consists of correspondence from forces on active service, civilians living in war zones, and even mail from one neutral country to another examined by one or both belligerents. The British forces even had special "Honour" envelopes, exempt from censorship at the regimental level though liable to examination by the base censor.

Censor Mark

Certified Mail

CENSUS MARKING. Postmark applied by cancelling machine to all correspondence passing through the post at certain times of the year to enable the Post Office to assess the volume of traffic being handled. In Britain the census mark takes the form of a diamond, occasionally with wavy obliterating lines or even a slogan alongside.

Census Marking (GB c. 1960)

CENTRED. Term applied to stamps to denote the position of the impression in relation to the perforations. Stamps in which the perforation is not so well aligned are said to be **Off Centre**.

Centred—good and poorly centred stamps

CERTIFIED MAIL. Mail for which a receipt is given to the sender and required from the addressee, but for which no hand-to-hand system of check exists in transit. This system, designed as a cheap but less secure alternative to **registration** was pioneered in the United States in 1955, a special 15c stamp being issued for the purpose. The system was subsequently adopted in Britain under the name of Recorded Delivery.

CERTIFYING STAMP. Cachet applied to official mail to certify that it is on government business and therefore entitled to pass through the post either free of charge or subject to some form of special inter-departmental account. This system developed in the United Kingdom in the aftermath of Uniform Penny Postage and continued until 1983. It was also imitated by many Commonwealth countries. *See also* Frank, Free Mail and Official Mail.

Certifying Stamp—Tower of London, Irish Dept. of Transport and Board of Trade

CHALK-SURFACED PAPER. Highly surfaced, chalk-coated paper introduced by De La Rue in 1902 and used for many British and colonial stamps. Any attempt to remove the postmark causes damage to the surface. For this reason also, great care should be taken not to soak such stamps, but to use a sweat box to remove backing paper. Chalk-surfacing may be detected by a silver pencil or coin which leaves a black mark. Although this coating is chiefly associated with De La Rue letterpress stamps, it was also used for photogravure stamps of 1963 (2s Holiday booklet), a printing of Manx 3d of the same year, and certain Elizabethan commemorative issues. ■

CHALKY PAPER. Sometimes loosely used as a synonym for **Chalk-Surfaced Paper** but more properly applied to the whiter paper introduced to British stamps in April 1962 to improve their appearance. This chalky paper does not respond to the silver test mentioned above.

CHARGE MARKS AND LABELS. Handstruck marks and adhesive labels applied to unpaid or underpaid mail or packets infringing postal regulations to explain the reason for the deficiency and the amount to be recovered from the recipient. Prior to the advent of Uniform Postage in 1839–40 it was the rule rather than the exception to post letters unpaid, so the amount of postage to be recovered from the sender was indicated in black ink, either manuscript or handstruck.

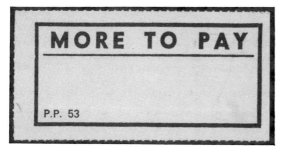

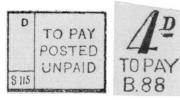

Charge Marks and Labels

CHARITY LABELS. Labels of a non-postal nature, sold by various bodies to raise funds, and affixed by their purchasers to letters and cards. The first fund-raising label was issued in Italy in 1860 on behalf of Garibaldi's Sicilian campaign; the first in Britain was issued in 1864–5 to raise money for the Shakespeare Memorial at Stratford. The most widely used charity labels are **Christmas seals**, but they have also been employed for an infinite variety of good causes.

Charity Labels

CHARITY STAMPS. Postage stamps bearing a premium in aid of some philanthropic object. Usually the amounts of postage and the charity premium are clearly and separately stated, but in some of the earliest issues (e.g. Queensland 1900) stamps sold for a shilling only prepaid a penny's postage, and the difference (11d) was credited to the charity. Many countries make special annual issues, such as the New Zealand **Health stamps**, the Dutch Summer stamps and **Children's stamps** and the Swiss **"Pro Juventute"** and **"Pro Patria"** issues. Great Britain issued postal stationery in 1890 to celebrate the Jubilee of Penny Postage. Envelopes sold for a shilling carried only 1d postage, the balance going to a charity for PO widows and orphans.

Check Letters—AK-BL on GB 1d. stamp of 1880

Charity Stamps

CHECK LETTERS. Letters in the lower corners of British stamps (1840) and repeated but in reverse order in the upper corners as well from 1858 onwards, as a precaution against "piecing" – the technique of matching up the unobliterated portions of two previously used stamps. Theoretically also a means of preventing forgery, it did not thwart the forgers of the Stock Exchange shilling (1870–3); of the 63 combinations of corner letters known, 15 are ones that could not exist in genuine stamps. Check letters were gradually discontinued in Britain between 1880 and 1902. They were also briefly (1850–7) used by Victoria, Australia.

CHEQUE STAMPS. Embossed **fiscal** stamps applied to cheques from 1855 to 1971 to denote the Stamp Duty payable on them. Similar stamps were also used in the British colonies and in 1898 they were utilised by the postal administration of British Central Africa (now Malawi) for postal purposes during a shortage of 1d adhesive postage stamps. These cheque stamps were overprinted "Internal Postage" to denote their postal usage.

CHILDREN'S STAMPS. Charity stamps bearing a premium in aid of children's charities. Stamps inscribed in Latin "Pro Juventute" have been issued for this purpose by Switzerland since 1913 and similar stamps, inscribed "Kinderzegels"

by Holland since 1924. More specific - and unusual - stamps have been issued by Costa Rica (for juvenile delinquents) and Grenada (milk for children). In more recent years the term has also been applied to stamps designed by children and issued by many countries since 1958.

CHOPS. Seals or handstamps bearing ideographs or Japanese characters, used to overprint stamps of territories occupied by Japanese forces during the Second World War.

Chops (Japan, Second World War)

CHRISTMAS CHARITY POST STAMPS. Stamps issued by Scout and church groups in Britain since 1981, the British Telecommunication Act of that year, permitting charities to carry Christmas and New Year cards between 25 November and 1 January each year.

Christmas Charity Post Stamp (GB, 1981)

CHRISTMAS SEALS. Charity labels invented by Einar Holboell and issued under the auspices of the postal administrations of Denmark, Norway and Sweden from 1904 onwards. They spread to the USA in 1907 and have since been adopted in many other countries to adorn Christmas greetings mail and raise money for charities, notably children's and anti-TB funds. Although they have no postal validity they often have quasi-official recognition, and in South Africa have even been sold in booklets in the same manner as postage stamps.

Christmas Seals (Denmark, 1904)

CHRISTMAS STAMPS. Special postage stamps, with or without a charity premium, issued for use on greetings cards at the Christmas season. Although Canada issued a stamp inscribed XMAS 1898 the first stamps actually intended for use on greetings cards were issued by Austria in 1937, followed by Hungary (1943), Cuba (1951) and Australia (1957). Britain introduced Christmas **aerogrammes** in 1965 and adhesive stamps in 1966. Costa Rica pioneered **compulsory stamps** for use on Christmas mail in 1959.

Christmas Stamps

CHROMOLITHOGRAPHY. Form of **lithography** using two or more colours simultaneously. The earliest stamps of this type were the Zurich cantonal issue of 1843, with red lines as a background to motifs printed in black. This process was not widely used, although notable examples of four-colour stamps include the Soroka **zemstvo** issue of 1879 and El Salvador's pair of 1897.

Chromolithography (El Salvador, 1897)

Cigarette Paper (Latvia, 1919)

Cinderella Stamp (Spanish Flag Day label)

Circular Datestamp (double and single ring)

CIGARETTE PAPER. Thin paper intended for rolling cigarettes, but used by Latvia for an issue of stamps in 1919.

CIGARETTE TAX STAMPS. Stamps indicating a government tax on cigarettes, but used provisionally as **postage due labels** at Durban and Fordsburg, South Africa in August–December 1922.

CINDERELLA STAMP. Virtually anything resembling a postage stamp, but not issued for postal purposes by a government postal administration and therefore usually omitted from the standard catalogues.

CIRCULAR DATESTAMP. Usually abbreviated as "cds" and denoting a form of postmark produced by single or combined (double-circle incorporating date and obliterating element) stamps. They date from the 1820s and have also been applied by machine since the 1880s.

CIRCULAR DELIVERY STAMPS. Stamps issued by private companies established in Britain in 1865–7 for the delivery of circulars, sample packets and other printed matter at rates which undercut the Post Office. These companies were suppressed following a law suit which found them to have infringed the Postmaster General's monopoly; but the Post Office was forced to concede cheaper postage in 1870.

CLASSIC. Term loosely applied to any stamps issued before 1875, as well as certain rarities of more modern vintage.

Circular Delivery Stamp (Edinburgh & Leith)

Classic Stamps—Belgium, France, Cape of Good Hope

CLEAN-CUT PERFORATIONS. Perforations which are sharply incised and have the punched discs of paper removed.

Clean-Cut Perforations (GB Edward VIII, 1936)

CLEANED. Stamps which have had their cancellation removed chemically either for re-use or for the purpose of philatelic fraud, either passing off as unused or mint, or as the basis for forged postmarks. ■

CLEANED PLATE. Printing plate clogged with ink due to frequent usage, then cleaned, will therefore produce stamps in quite different states. Philatelists can collect matched pairs of stamps from the same plate before and after cleaning.

Cleaned Plate (Greek stamp—before and after plate cleaning)

CLICHE. French term for a stereo or electro produced by direct or indirect casting, used in the **letterpress** process, but loosely applied to the individual components of a printing plate.

Climax Dater

Co-extensive Line (with plate number 17)

Cogwheel cancel (Bavaria, 1850–69)

CLIMAX DATER. Rubber datestamp used 1885–1935 at minor sub post offices in the UK. Originally intended solely for stamping postal orders, their use was extended to parcel labels (c. 1895) and ordinary mail (c. 1905). Because they had an average life of only 2–3 years, these datestamps are sometimes, though erroneously regarded by collectors as "temporary rubber datestamps", although some are known to have remained in use for upwards of 20 years. They were invariably struck in violet ink until 1911 when black ink was adopted, but violet and other colours are sometimes encountered right down to 1935 when they were superseded by steel datestamps.

CO-EXTENSIVE LINE. Jubilee line broken into short lengths, extending only to the height or breadth of the marginal stamps in the sheet.

COGWHELL CANCEL. Circular numbered obliteration used by Bavaria, 1850–69, so-called on account of the ratchet projections surrounding the numerals.

College Stamps (Oxford and Cambridge, 1871–86)

Coin Daté (14 November 1958)

Coil Stamps (Japan, imperf vertically)

COIL STAMPS. Stamps prepared in rolls or coils to be dispensed either from coin-operated slot machines, or from automatic devices used in firms' postrooms. Such stamps may differ from ordinary "sheet" stamps by (a) partial perforation, (b) sideways watermark, (c) coil joins – i.e. overlapping thicknesses of paper where strips are connected – or (d) some form of numerical **backprint** applied to every fifth or tenth stamp.

COIN DATÉ. French expression meaning "dated corner", applied to the corner blocks of French stamps which denote the actual date of printing.

COLLEGE STAMPS. Private stamps issued by certain colleges at Oxford and Cambridge Universities between 1871 and 1886 for their inter-college messenger services. This practice was suppressed by the Post Office, although some colleges continued to evade the regulations by producing special envelopes with embossed flaps. Keble College produced a label in 1970 to celebrate its centenary and these are known to have been used on college mail. Stamps were also produced by several American colleges to prepay local delivery fees, and by certain business schools as aids in commercial practice, the latter having no postal validity.

COLLOTYPE. Printing process using gelatine images of photographs employed to produce the Poltava zemstvo 1 kopek stamp of 1912. It is best known philatelically for the production of the souvenir sheet commemorating the 1950 London International Stamp Exhibition, with reproductions of famous **classics**. ■

COLOUR CHANGELING. A stamp which has changed colour due to chemical or climatic influences such as humidity or strong sunlight. British halfpenny stamps of 1900 and 1902–4, normally green, change to blue on exposure to sunlight. ■

COLOUR FAKE. A stamp whose colour has deliberately been changed by chemical means to convert a common to a rare shade. ■

COLOUR PROOF. Impression of a stamp taken in the approved colour or colours prior to the commencement of general production. ■

COLOUR TRIALS. Proofs taken of a stamp in a wide range of colours, or combinations of colours, to enable a postal authority to decide which colours to select for the issued stamps. ■

COLOURED PAPERS. Papers other than white have been extensively used in stamp production and consist of (a) paper to which dye has been added at the pulp stage and therefore coloured throughout (both front and back); (b) paper whose surface has been coloured after production (colour on front only, with a white back); or (c) tinted paper whose appearance is only slightly toned. The lastnamed may indicate some chemical added for security reasons, e.g. **Bleuté paper**. Some British stamps had the gummed side tinted to assist the printer and ensure that they were not printed on the gummed side. ■

COLOURED POSTMARKS. Strictly speaking, any postmarks applied in ink other than black. In Britain, black ink only became the norm in 1857 and before that date a wide range of colours was used. To this day, however, different colours are frequently used for rubber stamps. Multicoloured postmarks were pioneered by Czechoslovakia, 1935–40, two- or three-colour combinations being used. Three-colour postmarks were used in Britain at philatelic events in 1964 and 1970. ■

COMB PERFORATION. Perforation in which the perforating pins are arranged in a comb pattern – a long horizontal line with short vertical lines – so that the top and sides of a row of stamps may be perforated at one stroke. Usually identified by the evenness and regularity of the intersecting holes.

COMBINATION COVER. Cover bearing the stamps of more than one postal administration, where the stamps of each have prepaid the postage for a different section of the journey.

COMMATOLOGY. Pseudo-scientific word, used mainly in the United States, to denote the study of **postmarks** of all kinds (from the Greek word *Komma*, meaning a segment or cut).

COMMEMORATIVE LABELS. Adhesive labels designed to commemorate events, anniversaries and personalities and affixed to covers and postcards as souvenirs. The earliest labels, dating from 1845, were connected with exhibitions. The earliest non-exhibition label was issued in France in 1855 as propaganda for the Congregation du Sacre-Coeur. The earliest English commemorative label was issued in 1864 to mark the quatercentenary of William Shakespeare. Though largely superseded by **commemorative stamps** they are produced to this day for an infinite variety of events, usually too local in character to merit the issue of stamps.

Comb Perforation (New Zealand, Edward VII)

Combination Cover

Commemorative Labels (Philatelic Congress and London exhibition)

Commemorative Postage Stamps

Commemorative Postmark—1986 British Philatelic Federation Congress

COMMEMORATIVE POSTAGE STAMPS. Stamps designed to commemorate current or historic events and personalities and nowadays on sale for only a limited period. Many of the earliest commemoratives had restricted validity (e.g. a country's inland mail), as the practice was frowned on by the Universal Postal Union. Opinions differ as to what constituted the first commemorative issue, claims having been advanced for stamps of Baden and Wurttemberg (1851), New Brunswick (1860), France (1863) and Peru (1871); but any commemorative aspect in these issues was indirect or purely coincidental. The earliest example of deliberate commemoration was provided by the USA whose 3c stamped envelopes of 1876 celebrated the Centenary of Independence. The first adhesive commemorative was a 2pf of a Frankfurt-am-Main local post (1887), and the first government issue was the series of New South Wales celebrating the centenary of British settlement (1888).

COMMEMORATIVE POSTMARKS. Postmarks, either handstruck or applied by machine, intended to commemorate an event or anniversary. The earliest examples pertain to temporary post offices established at special events. Postmarks purporting to have been used at the International Exhibition London in 1851 are now known to be fakes, using the genuine handstamp of the 1862 Exhibition and a "51" date slug. The honour for having the earliest commemorative postmark, therefore, goes to France, which had special handstamps for use at the Exposition Universelle, Paris in 1855. The earliest

machine cancellation of this type was used in 1893 to celebrate the Columbian Exposiiton, while Canada used **flag cancels** in 1897 to celebrate the Diamond Jubilee of Queen Victoria.

COMMERCIAL PROPAGANDA. Advertising has often been incorporated in the sheet margins of stamps, or in the se-tenant coupons in booklet panes, but instances on actual stamps are much rarer. In 1923 Costa Rica overprinted the 5c definitive with a slogan advertising coffee, while Cuba has issued stamps advertising its tobacco and sugar products. Self-adhesive stamps of Sierra Leone were issued to publicise not only the country's diamond industry, but more specifically Harry Winston, the American jewellery company. Commercial advertising in slogan postmarks has been permitted by Italy and France. The British Post Office does not knowingly permit it, although a few instances are known where brand names and trademarks have appeared in sponsored postmarks.

COMMONWEALTH REPLY COUPONS. *See* International Reply Coupons.

COMPARTMENT LINES. Irregular lines outside the normal printed area of stamps, occurring in letterpress plates where extraneous metal "flashing" has not been removed in the manufacturing process and therefore picks up ink during printing. Such flaws are common on Australian stamps of 1914–23 and the New Zealand 1d Dominion issue.

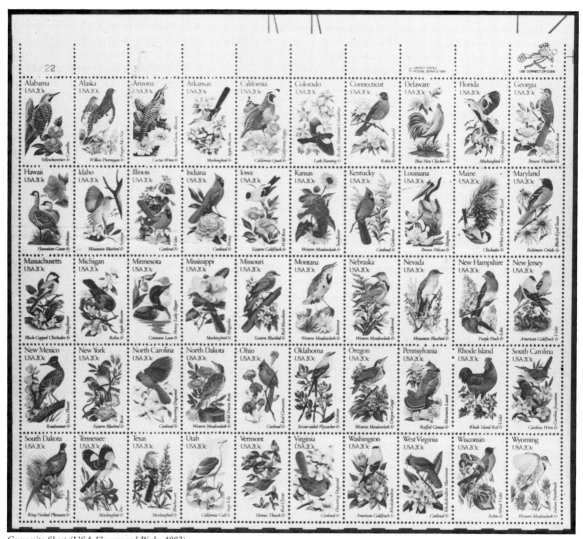

Composite Sheet (USA Flowers and Birds, 1982)

COMPOSITE SHEET. A sheet of stamps made up of different values, types or designs, or a normal sheet over-printed or surcharged in a similar manner, enabling a complete unit or set of stamps to be obtained from a single sheet. In modern practice, such stamps are usually arranged in joined (se-tenant) pairs, strips and blocks for cutting up and binding into **booklets.** Outstanding examples of composite sheets, however, include recent US sheets showing the flags, flowers and birds of the 50 states.

COMPOSITE STAMPS. Stamps in which the design is spread over two or more stamps. This technique was introduced by Poland (1957) for two 60gr stamps showing duelling fencers. Recent examples include the US block of four 2c stamps depicting the Cape Hatteras National Seashore Park (1972), the copra industry strip of five 48s stamps from the Tokelau Islands (1984) and the strip of five 12p for the 150th anniversary of the Liverpool and Manchester Railway, issued by Britain (1980).

Composite Stamps (GB Railways, 1980)

Compound of Perforation and Roulette (Papua New Guinea, 1969)

Compound Perforation (Canada, Bosnia)

COMPOUND ENVELOPE. Postal stationery envelope bearing more than one embossed or impressed stamp.

COMPOUND OF PERFORATION AND ROULETTE. Stamps using both of the principal methods of separation simultaneously, usually having horizontal perforations and vertical rouletting, or vice versa. Examples include the South Africa **bantams** of 1942–4, the Duttia quarter anna of 1912 and the Elema Art series of Papua New Guinea (1969).

COMPOUND PERFORATION. Perforation involving two or more different gauges on the same stamp. Many British stamps are perforated 15 x 14, i.e 15 horizontally, against the fibre of the paper, and 14 vertically. Compound perforation counteracts the tendency of sheets to split along the perforations according to the fibres of the paper.

COMPOUND ROULETTE. Form of pierced separation in which the gauge or pattern is not the same on all four sides of the stamp. Thus the Yugoslav "Chainbreakers" may be found with a compound of zigzag and straight-line roulette, while the British Consular Mail stamps of Madagascar are known imperforate at top and bottom, with straight- and arc-roulette at the sides.

COMPULSORY POSTAGE DUE LABELS. Postage due labels affixed to mail which has failed to use the compulsory charity stamps noted below. Special labels of this kind have been issued by Portugal, Rumania and Yugoslavia.

Compulsory Postage Due Labels (Portugal, Yugoslavia)

Compulsory Postage Stamps

COMPULSORY POSTAGE STAMPS. Charity stamps issued by some contries for compuslory use on mail posted on certain days. Portugal pioneered them from 1911 till 1928, but they were also issued by Greece (1914–56), Rumania (1915–36), Colombia (1935–70) and Ecuador (1920–61) and have been used by Yugoslavia since 1933. Many British colonies issued stamps during the First World War to denote a special wartime tax on mail. In more recent years special stamps have been issued by West Germany (for the Berlin airlift, 1949), Iraq and Bahrain (Palestinian relief), Cyprus (refugee relief, 1974–7) and India (Bangladesh refugee relief, 1971).

COMPULSORY REGISTRATION. Practice adopted by many postal administrations when coins, jewellery or other valuables are detected in ordinary, unregistered packets in transit. Such packets are then registered and handled more securely to their destination, but the registration fee and a fine are levied on the recipient. Special postmarks and labels have been used for this purpose by the British PO since 1862.

COMPUTATION OF OFFICIAL POSTAGE. Stamps have been issued by two countries for the purpose of computing the amount of postage due on official mail. Germany produced sets of stamps inscribed FREI DURCH ABLOSUNG for use in Prussia (1903) and Baden (1905), each set being used for 12 months in order to assess the amount of revenue owed to the imperial postal service for government mail carried. A similar device was used in Thailand in 1963–4. Stamps inscribed in Thai signifying "For Government service statistical research" were compulsorily used on official correspondence to determine the amount handled by the various departments.

Compulsory Registration—usually applied to unregistered mail containing coin

Computation of Official Postage (Germany, Thailand)

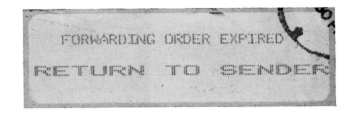

Computer-designed stamps—Netherlands (1970) and labels (USA word processor explanatory label)

Computer stamp (South Africa)

Concentration Camp Mail (Dachau-Allach Camp)

COMPUTER-DESIGNED STAMPS AND LABELS.
Micro-chip technology first affected philately in 1970 when the Netherlands issued a set of five stamps with spiral or geometric patterns produced by computer. In 1985 Martha Poppe designed a definitive series for Brazil in which the motifs were originated by dot-matrix printer. In recent years some Postage Paid Impressions have been produced by computer in conjunction with the addressing of packets used in mail-shots, while the explanatory labels now affixed to undeliverable mail in the United States have their inscriptions produced by dot-matrix printer from a word-processor.

COMPUTER STAMPS. Term sometimes used loosely as a synonym for **automatic stamps** or **Frama labels**, but more properly applied to stamps produced by micro-processor machines which weigh parcels and postal packets and calculate the appropriate amount of postage, which is then denoted by means of a gummed label indicating prepayment as well as giving the date and place of posting. Such computer stamps are now in use in South Africa, New Zealand, Singapore, Australia and Hong Kong.

CONCENTRATION CAMP MAIL. Mail from the concentration camps established by the Nazi regime in Germany and later in occupied Europe, distinguished by special postmarks, stationery and even stamps. An undenominated green label was issued in 1943 to allow the relatives of inmates of Theresienstadt camp to frank parcels addressed to the camp. The Jewish Council in Lodz ghetto were permitted to organise an internal post and issue stamps inscribed in German. In 1945 displaced persons housed in the former concentration camp at Dachau-Allach organised their own postal service and issued stamps and a miniature sheet with a premium in aid of the Red Cross. *See also* Prisoner of War Mail.

Concessionary Parcel Stamps (USA, Germany, Italy)

Continuous Overprint—Multiple Posthorns (W. Germany, 1948)

Condeminium—New Hebrides

CONCESSIONARY PARCEL STAMPS. Bipartite stamps issued by Italy since 1953, inscribed "Trasporto Pacchi in Concessione", and used by carriers and freight companies operating local parcel delivery services at rates lower than the government service. These stamps denote the payment of a small fee to the state for permission to operate the local services. Both Germany (1942–4) and the USA (1968) issued stamps to indicate concessionary rates in respect of servicemen's parcels.

CONCESSIONARY POSTAGE LABELS. Labels without postal validity, but denoting a special tax on letters and packets which the Italian Post Office has permitted private companies and agencies to transmit and deliver since July 1928. These labels are inscribed "Recapito Autorizzato" (Authorised Delivery).

CONDOMINIUM. Government shared by two or more powers over another territory, e.g. Canton Island (Anglo-American), the Sudan (Anglo-Egyptian) and the New Hebrides (Anglo-French). Only in the last case, however, have stamps been issued, thus inscribed and bearing captions in English and French respectively.

CONTINUOUS LINE. Jubilee line in the sheet margins of stamps extending without breaks, as opposed to Co-extensive lines.

CONTINUOUS OVERPRINT. A multiple, overall overprint, applied without regard to positioning on the individual stamps in a sheet. Good examples are the republican overprints of Spain (1931) and the multiple Posthorns of West Germany (1948).

CONTROL LETTERS. Letters inscribed in the sheet margins of some British stamps from 1881 onwards as an accountancy measure. From 1904 till 1947, when these controls were discontinued, they also incorporated numerals indicating the last digits of the year of issue.

CONTROL MARKS. Security endorsement by **overprint**, **underprint** or **perforation** applied to stamps used by institutions and firms to prevent pilferage.

CONTROL NUMBERS. Numerals engraved in the margins of plates used for the production of stamps in certain countries, notably Canada and the United States as a form of security over the plates that the printers received from the vaults for production. *See also* Current Numbers.

CONTROL OVERPRINTS. Overprints applied to stamps as a precaution in cases of theft and fraud. Good examples are Persian stamps of 1922 overprinted CONTROLE with the date, after quantities of high-value stamps leaked on to the philatelic market. US stamps were overprinted "Kans." or "Nebr." in 1929 for use in Kansas and Nebraska respectively, as an experimental measure to minimise losses from post office burglaries. Between 1856 and 1883 Mexican stamps were overprinted with district names and sub-district numbers to defeat the use of stamps stolen in transit. East Germany overprinted stamps with postal district names and numbers in 1948 as a temporary measure following the currency reform in the Anglo-American zones.

COPPERPLATE ENGRAVING. Alternative name for the **intaglio** process, so-called from the fact that copper plates were mainly used for this purpose.

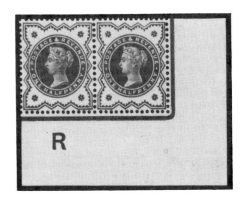

Control Letters (GB George V and Victoria issues)

*Control Overprints
(Mexico, East Germany)*

*Control Overprints—
Controle (Persia, 1922)*

CORK CANCELS. Obliterators roughly fashioned from corks were widely used in Canada and the United States in the mid-19th century, and were often carved into letters and pictorial motifs. The resulting postmarks are of immense interest to postal historians. Cork cancels, in a five-barred oval pattern, were used in the United Kingdom to obliterate stamps used on parcels (1883–5) and subsequently used on registered mail.

COUNTER COIL PAIR. Pair of stamps from dispensing machines used by post office counter clerks in New Zealand, the public having no direct access to them. The coils of 1956–7 were made up of sections and each section (of 24, 20 or 16 stamps) was divided by a gutter and numbered 1 to 19 in black ink to aid accounting. The decimal stamps from 1967 onwards have been in 20 sections of 10 (numbered 1 to 19) or 30 sections of 10 (numbered 1 to 29). The figures exist sideways, inverted, upwards or downwards in relation to the stamps. Philatelists collect these counter coils in pairs showing the numerals in the gutter.

Counter Coil Pair (New Zealand, 1967)

Cork Cancels—USA plain and fancy

COUNTERFOIL. Portion of a stamp or label retained by the sender as a receipt and the other portion affixed to the parcel card, or in some cases, to the packet itself. Italian parcel stamps (1914–54) had counterfoils inscribed "Sulla Ricevuta" to indicate their usage. In Britain, the counterfoils of postal orders can be datestamped by the office of issue - one method whereby collectors can obtain examples of the postmarks used at post office counters.

Coupon (Czechoslovakia, 1938)

Courier Services—label used on British government mail

Cover—satirical illustrated cover marking the 50th anniversary of US Social Security Act

COUPON. An attachment to a stamp which conveys additional information. Coupons are included to make up booklet panes, or may be incorporated in sheets for decorative or commemorative purposes. Czechoslovakia pioneered the latter technique in 1930, but it has also been widely used elsewhere. The **tabs** attached to many Israeli stamps are also a form of coupon.

COUPON PAPER. Grey **granite paper**, originally intended for wartime food coupons, used in 1919 by a Berlin printer in the production of stamps for Latvia. ∎

COURIER SERVICES. Special services operated by various governments for the transmission of official correspondence and forces' mail. Special postmarks and labels are provided in connexion with the British Forces' Courier Service, while special stamps were issued by the German Democratic Repub-

lic, inscribed or overprinted "Zentraler Kurierdienst" (Central Courier Service). Distinctive labels, cachets and stationery have been used by the inter-departmental courier services in Great Britain.

COVER. Envelope or wrapper for letters and packets. Stamps are said to be "on original cover" when retained intact on the envelope used in postal transmission. *See also* Campaign, Combination, Crash, First Day, First Flight, Patriotic, Stampless and Wreck covers.

COWALL CANCELLATION. *See* Hooded Datestamp.

CRACKED PLATE. Printing plate exhibiting cracks caused by undue pressure or general deterioration after long usage. Such cracks manifest themselves on stamps as white or coloured lines disturbing the impression.

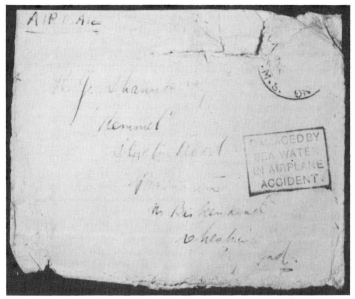

Crash Cover

SALVAGED MAIL
AIRCRAFT CRASH
PRESTWICK 25-12-54

GRANTHAM
RLY ACCIDENT

DAMAGED BY
SEA WATER
IN AIRPLANE
ACCIDENT

Markings used on crash covers recovered from railway and aircraft accidents

*Creased Transfer—
(Oldenburg, 1859)*

CRASH COVER. Postal cover salvaged from crashed aircraft and mail-trains. Such covers frequently bear the marks of fire or other damage, explained by special labels or cachets before onward transmission to the addressee. The earliest example of labels in this context was provided in the case of mail salvaged from the crash of the Grand Trunk Railway in Canada, 1873. The earliest example of special marking of mail salvaged from an air crash occurred in 1934 when letters recovered from an exploded mail rocket off the Scottish coast were endorsed by rubber stamp.

CREASED TRANSFER. A paper transfer in the lithographic process, which has been creased or distorted when laid down on the stone, producing compression or distortion in the impression. A good example is provided by the NFW variety in Newfoundland's 1c stamps of 1910.

CROSS. One of the commonest heraldic symbols, widely used in stamp design. Anonymous labels bearing a white cross on a red ground were used for **postage due** purposes in Switzerland, 1883–1924. Various forms of cross have been used in overprints, notably the First World War issues raising funds for the Red Cross. Crosses have also been used in watermarks, notably on German stamps. A cross in an oval was die-stamped on the backs of Swiss stamps of 1862. *See also* Maltese Cross, St Andrew's Cross.

CROSS ROULETTE. Otherwise known by the French term *Percé en croix*, it was used as a form of separation by Portuguese stamps for issue in Madeira, and also in Tasmania, 1864.

CROWNED CIRCLE POSTMARKS. Special postmarks consisting of a circle surmounted by a crown, used in many British colonies and postal agencies in the 19th century to denote mail prepaid in cash. These marks were usually applied in red ink and are much sought after as forerunners of adhesive stamps in these countries.

CUBIERTA. Spanish word for "covered", denoting labels attached to insured letters and packets in Colombia from 1865 to 1909. These large labels were inscribed "Certificacion" and embellished with the national flag, either lithographed or hand-painted. These labels were detached from the packets on delivery and handed back to the postman as a form of receipt. Cubiertas were also issued by several Colombian states, including Cundinamarca, Santander and Tolima.

CURRENCY STAMPS. Postage or fiscal stamps used as units of currency during shortages of subsidiary coinage. **Encased stamps** were used during the American Civil War and the First World War, but the concept was taken a stage further by Russia which re-issued postage stamps of the Romanov Terentenary series in 1915–17 printed on cardboard and having inscriptions on the reverse to signify their legal tender status on par with silver coinage. Stamps of this type were also issued by the Don Cossacks, and in the Crimea, Armenia and the Ukraine in 1918–20. Austria issued stamps printed on cardboard for the same purpose, in 1919–20, but did not use a special inscription. Stamps have also been affixed to cards for circulation as money, in Rhodesia (1900), Madagascar (1915) and Spain (1936), while stamps reprinted on card were used in Bundi (India) and the Philippines during the Second World War.

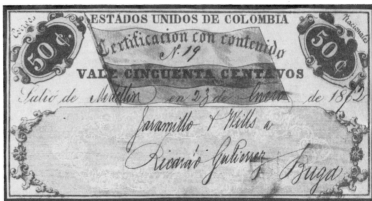

Cubierta (Colombian insured letter labels, 1865–1909)

Crowned Circle Postmarks (Antigua, Newfoundland, Havana, Trinidad)

Currency Stamps (Bundi (India), Russia, Austria, Spain)

CURRENT NUMBERS. Numbers inserted in the plate margins of some British and early colonial stamps to indicate the order in which the plates were manufactured. These numbers were quite distinct from the **control** or **plate numbers**.

Current Number (Lagos, 1886)

CUSTOMS INSPECTION LABELS AND MARKS. Adhesive labels and handstruck marks used by the postal section of Customs to indicate that parcels and packets coming from abroad have been examined for dutiable articles. Labels are used for resealing such packets, to indicate that examination has been concluded, and to show the amount of duty and other charges to be recovered from the recipient. Many countries use a variant of the green label C1, introduced by the Universal Postal Union in 1920, as a form of declaration for letters and small packets to prevent delay in Customs examination. A facsimile of this label is used by Guernsey as a handstruck mark for the same purpose. *See also* Franc de Droits.

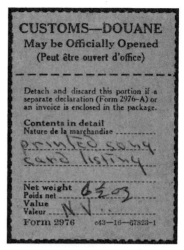

Customs Declaration and Inspection Labels

CUT-OUTS. Embossed or impressed stamps on postal stationery, cut out and used as adhesives. This practice is sanctioned by many postal administrations, enabling the public to utilise stamps from stationery which has been spoiled. The use of cut-outs has been permitted in Britain since 1905.

Cut-outs—George VI postal stationery stamp used on piece

Cut Square—GB Queen Victoria 10d. embossed

Cut to Shape—postal stationery stamps

Cylinder Numbers—single-colour and multicoloured stamps

CUT SQUARE. Embossed stamps, such as those of India (1854) and Britain (1847–54), cut in the form of a rectangle.

CUT TO SHAPE. Embossed stamp, as above, or from postal stationery, trimmed close to the outline of the impression. Old-time collectors often cut their specimens in this manner to fit the printed spaces in their stamp albums.

CYLINDER NUMBERS. Tiny numbers engraved on the cylinders used in the photogravure process and usually appearing in the margin of sheets of stamps thus printed. British stamps are usually printed in two panes similarly numbered, but distinguished by a dot after the number in the right-hand pane.

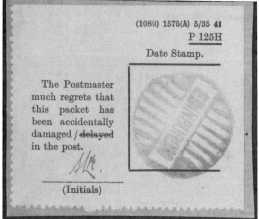

Damaged Mail—GB labels for damaged and 'found loose' mail

DAMAGED MAIL. Mail damaged in transit includes **crash** and **wreck covers**, but there are other less dramatic instances in which letters, parcels and packets may suffer damage. Special labels and cachets have been used by many postal administrations to signify all kinds of damage, ranging from fire caused in post boxes by vandals, to accidental immersion in water. Packets and parcels which have burst open are treated as "broken packets", and distinctive postmarks thus inscribed, as well as re-sealing labels, have been used.

DANDY ROLL. Wire-gauze roller which impresses the paper with its texture (e.g. "wove" or "laid") as the pulp leaves the vats. The wire or metal bits are woven or soldered on the dandy roll to produce **watermarks** in the paper.

DATAPOST. Name used by the British Post Office for an express service introduced in 1971, guaranteeing next-day delivery in any part of the United Kingdom. This service has since been linked with similar services in many other countries, such as Priority Mail (Canada) and Express Mail (USA). A feature of these international services is the use of labels with a uniform logo and stationery in a distinctive orange and blue livery. Various labels associated with Datapost include one for use on the trans-Atlantic service by Concorde.

DATE CUTS. Vertical cuts in the **Jubilee line** below stamps printed at Somerset House in 1911–12. One cut under the last stamp indicates the 1911 printing, while two denote the 1912 printing. Similar cuts may be found on other letterpress stamps of the Edwardian and Georgian periods, some of which were undoubtedly applied deliberately by the printers. These plate markings are of considerable interest to philatelists and are very useful in identifying the different plates.

DATED CORNER. *See* Coin Date.

DATED STAMPS. Stamps which incorporate the date of manufacture in their design. The earliest stamps to show the date of manufacture were the "Tigers" of Afghanistan which bore Moslem dates, changed each year. Many Canadian stamps from 1935 onwards included the year in their design in minuscule numerals. Marginal dating of stamps was first used by the People's Republic of China in 1952, although serial numbers serving a similar purpose had been used since 1950. Marginal dates were adopted by Italy (1955) and Austria, Hungary and West Germany (all 1969). Since 1973 all Brazilian stamps have prominently featured the last two digits of the year of issue after the country name. A recent ruling of the Universal Postal Union will make the inclusion of the date mandatory in all special issues from 1987 onwards.

DATESTAMPS. Implements for applying a date to postal matter. The term is also loosely used to denote the **postmarks** made by these instruments.

DEAD LETTER. Post Office term for an item of mail undeliverable because the address is incomplete or because the addressee is deceased or untraceable. Special labels and postmarks are used by many postal administrations on such mail before returning it to sender. *See also* Returned Mail, Undeliverable Mail.

Datapost—GB label used on Datapost mail sent on Concorde

Dated Stamps (Brazil, China)

DECOUPAGE. French term denoting a means of adjusting the pressure of the printing plate by "cut-outs" or built-up overlays to obtain lighter or deeper impressions as required. Misalignment results in exaggerated light or dark patches. ■

DEFERENTIAL CANCELLATION. Postmark designed in such a way that when a stamp was cancelled the effigy of the ruler was not defaced. Ornamental cancellations designed to frame the portrait were used by Spain, Sicily and the Indian state of Bhor.

Deferential Cancellation (Bhor (Indian State), Sicily)

DEFINITIVE STAMP. A stamp issued for ordinary postal purposes and placed on sale for an unlimited period. The term "permanent series" is often used by postal administrations to denote such stamps, as opposed to commemorative, charity and other special issues.

Definitive Stamp (Australia, 1939)

DELACRYL. Name invented by De La Rue to signify a printing process tailored specifically to stamp production and incorporating the major features of **lithography, photogravure, intaglio** and **letterpress**.

Delacryl—GB stamp printed by this process (1969)

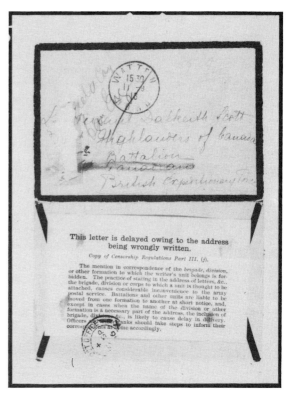

Delayed Mail—Wrongly Addressed

DELAYED MAIL. Mail held up in transmission through the post and thus indicated by means of labels, cachets or manuscript endorsement. The commonest cause of delay is missending, either as a result of careless sorting, or because of illegible addressing; but during the Second World War the British Post Office used **cachets** inscribed "Delayed by Enemy Action" to signify mail held up by air raids. Special labels and marks were also applied to correspondence which was held up in Europe during the German occupation and not delivered till the cessation of hostilities.

DELIBERATE ERROR. Error perpetrated by a postal administration to defeat philatelic speculation. When some Greek Red Cross stamps were discovered in 1937 with an inverted overprint, the Greek Post Office ordered a large quantity of inverts for sale at main post offices to prevent philatelic speculation. The USPO ordered the reprint of the

Deliberate Error—USA Hammarskjold inverted yellow, 1962

Dag Hammarskjold stamp of 1962 with the background colour inverted, to forestall the sale of a sheet as a major philatelic rarity. An attempt to repeat this, when the Canal Zone 4c Thatcher Ferry Bridge stamp was discovered with the bridge omitted, failed when the possessor of the genuine errors obtained a Supreme Court injunction against the USPO. Errors have also been deliberately perpetrated by unscrupulous printers for sale to collectors, e.g. Georgia (1921) and the Dominican Republic (1900).

DELIVERY TAX STAMPS. Spanish **postage due labels** issued in 1931 but later authorised for use as ordinary postage stamps.

DEMONETISED. Stamps withdrawn from circulation and deprived of any further postal validity. Such stamps are sometimes sold to dealers as **remainders.** Sometimes these stamps are overprinted to indicate their status, e.g. French "Annule" or German "Ausser Kurs".

DEPARTMENTAL STAMPS. Stamps provided for the use of government departments on official mail. Stamps overprinted for this purpose were issued by South Australia (1868–74), the United Kingdom (1882–1904) and Argentina (1913–38). The United States issued distinctive stamps for each of the nine executive departments (1873–9). Distinctive stamps have been provided by the New Zealand Post Office for the use of the Government Life Insurance Department since 1891.

DIAMOND ROULETTE. Otherwise known in French as *percé en losanges*, this form of separation takes the form of diamonds or lozenges with open corners.

Demonetised (Switzerland, AUSSER KURS = Out of Circulation)

Departmental Stamps—GB Army Official and New Zealand Life Insurance Dept

Diamond Roulette—Bulgaria 'lozenge' or diamond-shaped perforation

DICKINSON PAPER. Security paper with coloured silk threads enmeshed, invented by John Dickinson of Croxley and used in the production of British postal stationery (1841) and the 10d and 1s embossed adhesive stamps (1847–8). Similar silk-thread paper was used for some of the early issues of the German States and Switzerland.   ■

DIE. The original piece of metal or other material on which the stamp's design is first engraved and from which reproductions are made to form the printing unit. When a die is altered the original is called Die I and later versions Die II, III, etc, to differentiate them. Stamps printed form such dies are also given these designations by philatelists.

DIE PROOF. An impression pulled on special paper or card from the die, usually as a preliminary measure to check that all the detail is correct. Proofs taken by the engraver at various stages of the work are termed progress proofs.   ■

DIE-STAMPING. Alternative term for **Embossing**.

DIPLOMATIC MAIL. Correspondence which is transmitted by diplomatic bag for security reasons and invariably denoted by **certifying stamps** and special cachets, such as "By Bag", or identifying the embassy or consulate.

An original stamp die

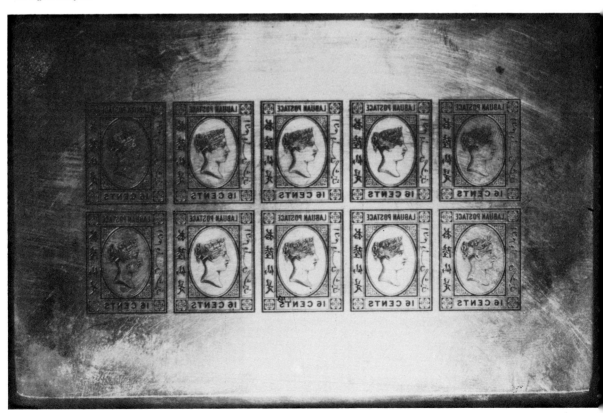

Directional Mark—'UNDELIVERED FOR REASON STATED/RETURN TO SENDER' (plus undeliverable mail label)

DIRECTIONAL MARK. Otherwise known as a Directory Mark (American), it is a **cachet** applied by a post office to undeliverable mail to indicate its ultimate disposal, usually for return to sender. *See also* Returned Mail, Undeliverable Mail.

DISCOUNT POSTAGE. Stamps printed, underprinted or overprinted to denote sale at a discount. Turkish stamps overprinted with an Arabic B (*Behie* = discount) were sold to business firms at a reduction of 20 per cent off face value for use on overseas mail, to encourage people to use the Turkish PO rather than the various foreign postal agencies. Persian stamps overprinted "Relais" were supplied to heads of post-stages at a discount, the overprint preventing them from reselling them to businessmen at the full price. In recent years Sweden and the UK have issued stamps in booklets at a discount. The Swedish stamps were introduced in 1979 and sold in booklets of 20 for 20kr but each represented 1.30kr worth of postage. British discount stamps had a letter "D" printed on the back, and later a five-pointed star to distinguish them from the normal full-price stamps.

Discount Postage (Sweden Privatpost, 1981)

DISINFECTED MAIL. Letters fumigated at quarantine stations on arrival from plague-ridden countries. In Britain the treatment of such mail was strictly governed by the Quarantine Act of 1710. Four methods of disinfection were used: (a) opening the letter to expose the contents to the air, (b) fumigation over a brazier, resulting in scorch marks, (c) splashing or dipping in vinegar (stains) and (d) piercing to let out the pestilential air (slits or cuts). Special marks were applied to such mail in France, Italy, Malta and other maritime countries in the 18th and early 19th centuries.

DOCKWRA MARK. Triangular handstruck mark denoting the prepayment of postage, devised by William Dockwra in connexion with his London Penny Post of 1680–2. Not only did Dockwra invent the world's first handstruck postage stamps now extant, but he also invented **postmarks** which gave the exact hour of posting – a device which the British Post Office did not revive till 1895!

DOCTOR BLADE. The flexible steel blade which removes surplus ink from the printing cylinder on high-speed modern presses. Faulty operation can cause flaws of a non-persistent nature on the printed stamps, taking the form of coloured lines.

DOMINICAL LABELS. Small detachable labels attached to the foot of Belgian stamps from 1893 to 1914, bearing the instruction in French and Flemish "Do not deliver on Sunday." Persons who did not object to the Sunday delivery of mail merely detached these labels before posting letters and cards. A similar inscription was printed on postal stationery, to be deleted by the sender where applicable.

DOUBLE IMPRESSION. A stamp in which some portion, or more rarely the whole image, has been doubly printed, due to a slight shift in the paper during the printing process.

Dockwra Mark (L = Lime Street)

Disinfected Mail

Dominical Label—Ne pas livrer le dimanche . . .

Doctor Blade Purple flaw on South African stamp

Double Letter—GB Penny Red, alphabet letter 'P' doubled

Double Paper (imitation)

Double Stamps—usually referred to as 'Duplex' (1850s–1920s)

DOUBLE LETTER. Prior to 1840 letters in Britian were charged double postage if they consisted of two sheets of paper, the envelope, if used, counting as a second sheet. Such letters were termed Double Letters and charged accordingly. The expression was often endorsed on the wrapper to indicate that double postage was due. The term is also used to denote **check letters** on some British line-engraved stamps where weak lettering was partially erased and re-punched, resulting in a partial double impression.

DOUBLE-LINED LETTERS. Outline letters forming **watermarks**, usually with the papermaker's name and/or trade mark.

DOUBLE PAPER. Security paper patented by C.F. Steel about 1870 and employed in the printing of some American stamps of the 1873 series. The paper consisted of two very thin sheets bonded together. Any attempt to clean off the cancellation would result in the destruction of the surface.

DOUBLE PRINT. The Swedish 20 ore stamp of 1876 was printed in a very pale orange colour which faded so badly that the sheets were withdrawn and printed a second time in vermilion, over the original impression. On sheets which were inaccurately registered both impressions are visible. This double print should not be confused with a **double impression**.

■

DOUBLE STAMP. The correct Post Office term for the type of handstamp sometimes described loosely by collectors as a **Duplex**. As the name implies, a double stamp is one in which the dater and obliterator are two quite separate components, often detachable from each other, but mounted in the same handle. Double stamps were in use from the early 1850s until the end of the century, although a few continued in use till the 1920s. Double stamps are widely used to this day by the smaller post offices in the United States and Canada.

DROP LETTER. A postal packet delivered to an address within the same postal delivery area as the office in which it was posted. Such letters, in the USA and some other countries, are conveyed at specially low rates of postage.

Dropped Letters

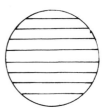

Dumb Cancellation—often used in wartime

Duplex Cancellations—integrated dater and obliterator

Duty Plate—key plate section obliterated to show duty plate

DROPPED LETTER. A letter forming part of a typeset inscription or overprint, which has dropped out of alignment with the others.

DRY PRINT. A stamp having a weak or thin appearance, due to the paper being too dry for the intaglio process, the printing ink being insufficiently fluid, or from the cylinder or plate having been too severely wiped before printing. ■

DUMB CANCELLATION. Obliteration which bears no indication of the office of origin. Many of the earliest cancellations, such as the **Maltese Cross** came into this category, although the term is applied more specifically to the mute "killers" of the late-19th century, and those handstamps of both World Wars which were applied to naval mail for security reasons to conceal their port of entry. *See also* Blackout Cancel.

DUPLEX CANCELLATION. Postmark made from a duplex handstamp, one in which the dater and obliterating element are integrated, as opposed to the separate components of **double stamps**. The earliest cancellations of Britain and Ireland, used experimentally between 1853 and 1860, were true duplexes and include such celebrated examples as the Rugby Shoe and Glasgow's "Madeleine Smith", so-called on account of its connexion with the famous murder trial of 1857.

DUTY PLATE. The plate used to print the value, or the name and value, on stamps printed at two operations. A separate duty plate is required for each denomination, but the plate which prints the general design is constant throughout and is called the **Head** or **Key Plate**.

ECONOMY GUM. Known in Germany as *Spargummi*, it was a type of gum applied in patterns or blobs to the backs of some stamps issued in the immediate aftermath of the Second World War. This was sufficient for the stamps to adhere to envelopes but cut the actual amount of gum required by almost 50 per cent.

ELECTRIC EYE MARKS. Marginal marks on sheets of stamps to ensure accurate perforation, alignment being controlled by a photo-electric device – the "Electric Eye" which scans the marks.

EMBOSSING. Otherwise known as Die-stamping, it is strictly speaking a method of stamping in relief rather than a printing process, although allied to print in the production of postage stamps and postal stationery. The relief or raised impression is obtained by placing the paper between two matching dies, one (male) bearing the design image in relief, the other having the (female) counterpart of the image in recess. The usual form of embossing is clear (or blind) as opposed to coloured. This process was first used philatelically in 1838, for the New South Wales letter sheets of the Sydney local post. It was used for the British postal stationery of 1841 and extended to adhesive stamps in 1845 (Basle "Dove"). Though extensively used in the 19th century it has been sparingly used in more recent times, other than for the Queen's head on some British special issues of 1968–73.

EN ÉPARGNE. French term meaning "in relief", used to describe the type of printing plate used in the **letterpress** process.

Electric Eye Marks—USA and GB stamps

Embossing

ENAMELLED PAPER. Highly glazed paper coated with a mixture of zinc white and glue, producing a very glossy but rather brittle surface. It was mainly used for printing stamps of Portugal and colonies. ■

ENCASED POSTAGE STAMPS. Stamps inserted in small rectangular or circular cases, with a transparent front and metal back, were used as small change during the American Civil War (1861–5) when there was a shortage of coins. The cases were devised by John Gault, a Boston sewing-machine salesman, who made a fortune from selling advertising space on the backs of the metal cases. The idea was revived at the end of the First World War in France, Germany and other European countries going through a similar period of coin shortage.

ENGINE-TURNING. Ornamental security device produced by means of a rose-engine or lathe patented by Jacob Perkins and used by the firm of Perkins, Bacon as the intricate background to the British line-engraved stamps of 1840–80. The intricate geometric pattern produced by the rose-engine made it impossible for anyone to forge such stamps. Engine-turning was also a characteristic feature of many of the colonial stamps produced by the same firm.

ENGRAVER'S PROGRESS PROOFS. Impressions taken by the engraver from a die while work is in progress, to check the development of the design. Such proofs may begin with the merest outline and gradually build up to the finished die. They are of immense interest to the collector as showing how a design was evolved. ■

ENTIRE. An envelope, postcard or wrapper, with stamps affixed or printed on it to prepay postage, and in complete condition.

ENTIRE LETTER. A complete folded letter sheet, with the communication on the inside and address on the outside, together with relevant postal markings and adhesive stamps, if relevant.

ENVELOPE. Form of wrapper or cover for letters, with the four corners of the sheet folded across the back. Sheets for envelopes were sold unfolded until the early 1840s when De La Rue invented a folding machine. Envelopes were used in Europe but very seldom postally in Britain where they counted as a second sheet and therefore doubled the postage rate. After 1840, however, and the advent of Uniform Postage, envelopes rapidly gained in popularity and had ousted the letter sheet by 1860.

Engine-turning

Entire—airmail cover from Falkland Islands, 1953

EPREUVE DE LUXE. French term meaning "luxury proof", signifying limited editions of **die proofs** produced by the government printing works either for presentation purposes or for sale to collectors.

ERASED. Term describing the removal of a portion of a design or overprint in order to modify it. A good example is provided by the first Australian **postage due labels** which were produced from plates previously used by New South Wales, the letters NSW being erased from the plates. Labels may be found with parts of the letters NSW at the foot.

Erased—error 20 PIASTRE instead of 2 PIASTRE; value (Corrientes, 1867); partly—BAYERN erased to allow for overprinting

ERINNOPHILY. Hybrid, pseudo-scientific word, from German *erinnerung* (commemoration) and Greek *philos*, love, to mean the study and collection of **commemorative labels**.

ERROR. A stamp which, inadvertently, has something wrong about its design, or some technical feature, but which has been issued by a postal authority. Not to be confused with flaws or **varieties** which occur during printing, due to faulty workmanship. The commonest type of error involves mistakes in the detail of the design. Sometimes these errors of detail or inscription are subsequently corrected, so that matched pairs of errors and corrections can be formed. Errors of colour arise either from the wrong colour being used for an entire sheet, or more probably a **cliche** of one value has been inserted in a **forme** of another and therefore appears in the colour of the latter. Paper error arises where stamps are printed on paper bearing a watermark or some other security feature, normally associated with another value. Perforation error arises from the use of a gauge not normally employed for that stamp. Printing errors arise from feeding the paper through a press inverted, reversed, reversed and inverted, or twice. Two-colour stamps are prone to such errors, which manifest themselves as inverted centres. Overprint and surcharge errors are common, and arise from the insertion of sheets of stamps upside down in relation to the overprint plate; or there may be mistakes in the typesetting of the overprint, involving inverted letters or numerals, the wrong fount, etc. Watermark errors are those in which the watermark is inverted or reversed by accident, or contains a device inserted by error on the **dandy roll**. *See also* Deliberate Error.

Error—design error, Cape Bauld and Cape Norman transposed (Newfoundland, 1928)

ESSAY. A design which has been submitted for a stamp, but not adopted, or has been adopted after alterations have been made. The earliest stamp essays were those submitted in connexion with the Treasury Competition of 1839.   ■

ETIQUETTE. French word for "ticket" or "sticker" and thus applied loosely to any label, but specifically used by collectors to signify **Airmail labels**.

EUROPA STAMPS. Stamps issued since 1956 with the word EUROPA (Europe) prominently inscribed thereon. The earliest issues were made by the six countries belonging to the European Coal and Steel Community, later the European Common Market or EEC, and used similar designs. In 1960, however, the Europa concept was taken over by the Conference of European Posts and Telecommunications Authorities and thereafter was used for the stamps issued annually by CEPT member countries. Uniform designs were used until 1974 when it was decided that stamps should be issued in a common theme, whose interpretation was left to individual countries. These stamps also incorporate the four interlocking posthorns logo of CEPT.

EXAMINERS' MARKS AND LABELS. These are applied to postal packets to denote examination by **censors** in time of war and unrest, or by **Customs** authorities . Marks are also applied sometimes, mainly to printed matter transmitted at special reduced rates of postage, to ensure that the regulations governing such classes of mail are being complied with. For this purpose the British Post Office, for example, used a series of small triangular marks. A wide variety of other marks, however, was employed from the late 18th century onwards during inspection of mail, ranging from the crowned royal monograms (up to 1840) to the initials and symbols employed in the check on Official Paid mail to ensure that only bona fide government correspondence was being transmitted.

EXHIBITION LABELS AND POSTMARKS. Exhibitions have provided the earliest known examples of both commemorative labels (1845) and special postmarks (1855). Philatelic exhibitions alone have produced a wealth of such collectable material since 1881, when a stamp show was held in Vienna. In the century since the first international philatelic exhibition at Antwerp in 1887, well over 100 shows of this type alone have produced a vast array of labels, postmarks, and, in more recent years, stamps and **souvenir sheets**.

Europa stamps

Examiners' Marks

Exhibition Label (London 1980 International Stamp Exhibition) and Postmark (France, 1855)

Exiled Government Posts

Expedition Stamps—usually overprints

EXILED GOVERNMENT POSTS. Postal services operated by governments forced to flee into exile temporarily in time of war. The Belgian government was forced into exile by the German occupation in 1914 and was established at Le Havre on French soil. Belgian stamps were used, but can be distinguished by their postmark. In 1916 the Serbian government took refuge in Corfu, Greece and used French stamps overprinted POSTES SERBES. Similar French stamps were used by the Montenegrin government in exile at Bordeaux in 1916. The Czech Legions issued their own stamps at Irkutsk, Siberia in 1919–20. During the Second World War stamps were printed in England for the use of the governments of Poland, Czechoslovakia, the Netherlands, Norway and Yugoslavia, used by embassies, military units and ships at sea. In some cases these exile stamps were used in the actual countries after liberation. The Polish exiles, in fact, used special French stamps (1939–40), stamps printed in Britain by Bradbury, Wilkinson or De La Rue (1941–5), a 50 kopek stamp at Jangi-Jul, Russia (1942) and stamps in Italian currency at Bari (1944).

EXPEDITION STAMPS. Stamps produced for the use of scientific or exploratory expeditions include those authorised by New Zealand in 1908 and 1911 for the Shackleton expedition to King Edward VII Land and the Scott expedition to Victoria Land respectively. An issue of British stamps suitably overprinted for the Shackleton-Rowatt Expedition of 1922 was aborted following the death of Sir Ernest Shackleton. More recent issues have included China's issue for Sven Hedin's expedition (1932) and the Falkland Islands Dependencies set overprinted for the Trans-Antarctic Expedition of 1955–8. Stamps for military expeditions include Indian stamps overprinted for the China Expeditionary Force (1900), Liberian stamps overprinted LFF for the Field Force sent against a native uprising (1915), the stamps of the Indian Expeditionary Force and Anglo-French Force to Togoland and Cameroons (1914), the Nyasaland Field Force (1918), the British stamps overprinted for East African and Middle East Forces (1942–3) and Indian stamps overprinted for use of UN forces in Korea, Indo-China, the Congo or Gaza (1953–65).

EXPERIMENTAL DUPLEX CANCELLATIONS. Special handstamps combining a dater and obliterating element, used experimentally in Britain and Ireland between 1853 and 1860. The types used in England and Wales had oval or circular obliterators, while Irish types were diamond-shaped. Some of the English stamps have acquired nicknames, such as the Reading Biscuit and Rugby Shoe, on account of the unusual shape of their postmarks. The Scottish types had rectangular obliterators with double-arc, circular or rectangular daters, the lastnamed including the celebrated "Madeleine Smith" stamps. *See also* Double Stamp.

EXPERIMENTAL ROULETTE. Form of trial stamp-separation devised by Henry Archer in 1847–8, prior to the invention of **perforation**. Another form of experimental roulette, known as the "Gladstone" or "Treasury Roulette", was tested in 1853–4.

EXPLANATORY LABELS AND MARKS. Devices used by postal authorities to give reasons for surcharging unpaid, underpaid or "infringement" mail, or to give the reasons for non-delivery, mis-sending, delay or damage in transit.

Explanatory Labels

Experimental Duplex cancellations—including the famous 'Madelaine Smith'

EXPLODED BOOKLET. A stamp booklet which has been taken apart so that the individual panes as well as the interleaving and covers can be fully displayed. This practice may be feasible when booklets are stapled, but is not recommended in the case of stitched booklets, as the components cannot be put together again without irremediable damage to the binding.

Exploded Booklet—front and back covers, pane of stamps and interleaving bearing advertising material

Express Airmail (Italy)

EXPRESS AIRMAIL. Special stamps for air express services have been issued by Italy, Canada, Colombia and the USA, while special cachets thus inscribed were used by Britain in 1920–1.

EXPRESS LABELS. Adhesive labels, usually printed in bright colours, have been provided by many countries to denote express and special delivery mail since the 1890s. British labels for ordinary express mail were printed in black on bright red paper. Labels for mail to be conveyed by post office messenger all the way were printed in red on white. Special delivery labels were printed in shades of brown or purple. In recent years labels in violet have been used for the Royal Mail Special Delivery service, and in blue, or orange and blue, for **Datapost.** Distinctive labels have also been provided for Expresspost and Swiftair, other forms of express service operated by the British PO in recent years.

Express Labels (also EXPRESS handstamp)

EXPRESS NEWSPAPER AND PRINTED MATTER POST. Stamps for the express delivery of newspapers and commercial printed matter have been issued by Czechoslovakia.

Express Newspaper and Printed Matter (Czechoslovakia)

EXPRESS PARCEL POST. Stamps for use on express parcels were issued by the Vatican in 1931.

Express Parcel Post (Vatican City, 1931)

Express Stamps

EXPRESS STAMPS. Distinctive postage stamps denoting the fee payable in respect of accelerated mail subject to special handling, either by the delivery office, or all the way. Services of this type have been in existence since the 18th century, but in their modern form date from 1839 when William F. Harnden of Boston formed an express delivery company. Special stamps of a local nature were issued by many American express companies, but the first government issue for this purpose was produced by the USPO in 1885. Stamps inscribed SPECIAL DELIVERY or EXPRESS, or their equivalents in other languages, were later issued by Canada (1898), New Zealand, Italy and Mauritius (all 1903), China, Spain (1905) and Mexico (1919).

FACSIMILE. An imitation of a genuine stamp, sometimes differing quite obviously from the original, and invariably marked in some way to denote its true status. Facsimiles are thus produced without intention to deceive or defraud, unlike **forgeries**.

Facsimile—US Newspaper stamp (overprinted FACSIMILE)

FAKE. A genuine stamp which has been altered or repaired in some way to make it appear what it is not, for the purpose of deceiving collectors. Stamps may be faked by cleaning or removing their cancellation, by altering the shade or colour chemically, by regumming stamps which have lost their gum, or by reperforating stamps which have had their original perforations trimmed, or which were released imperforate.

Fake—normal wing-margined stamp and similar stamp with margin removed and fake perforation added

Fakes also include damaged or defective stamps which have been repaired. *See also* Colour Changeling.

FANCY TYPE. Printer's type in some decorative style, used either in overprints or **typeset** stamps.

Fancy Type

FARLEY'S FOLLIES. American stamps of 1934–7 originally released imperforate on the authority of the Postmaster General, James A. Farley, and thus nicknamed by indignant collectors whose protests eventually forced the USPO to make such imperforates freely available to the philatelic market.

Farley's Follies—imperforate US issues, 1934–7

FIELD POST OFFICE. A post office established for the use of troops on active service. Such offices use postmarks thus inscribed or the abbreviation FPO, often with a number identifying the location. The earliest British FPOs operated within the UK during the annual manoeuvres, but since the Egyptian campaign of 1884 they have operated with the military forces in every part of the world, in peace and war.

Field Post Office cancellation

First Day Cover–Swedish 1985 Christmas stamps

FIRST DAY COVER. A cover bearing postage stamps postmarked and sent through the post on the first day they were officially authorised for use. Special **postmarks** have been used for this purpose in many countries since the late 1930s.

FIRST FLIGHT COVER. A cover which has been carried on the first mail flight between two points and which can be identified as such by either the **postmarks** thereon, or by some special **cachet**.

First Flight Cover—Wick to Kirkwall (Orkney Is.), 1934

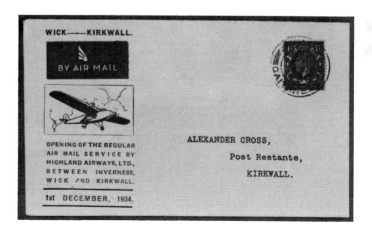

FISCAL STAMPS. Stamps intended for the collection of taxes, fees and duties for the revenue of the state, as opposed to those intended primarily for postal or telegraphic purposes. Such stamps which are subsequently permitted for postal use are said to be **Postal Fiscals**. Conversely unified stamps (i.e. those inscribed for postage and revenue) used for non-postal purposes would be regarded as fiscals.

Fiscal Stamps—for revenue use. Probably more fiscal stamps have been issued than postage!

FLAG CANCEL. Machine cancellation pioneered by the United States from 1894 onwards in which the obliterator takes the form of a waving Stars and Stripes. The seven wavy lines of this flag were later adopted as the obliterating element in many machines all over the world. Flag cancellations were also used by Canada (1897–1900), France (1898–1900), New Zealand (1899), Germany and Italy. A more recent variant of this was the "I'm Backing Britain" slogan used in the UK in 1968.

FLAMME ILLUSTREE. French term, derived from the oriflamme or heraldic guidon of medieval knights, and signifying pictorial **slogan postmarks** widely used in France since 1950 to publicise tourist resorts.

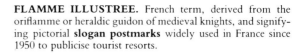

Flamme Illustree—French pictorial slogan postmarks

FLAW. A fortuitous blemish upon the design of a stamp or its perforation, which has arisen in the course of manufacture. Such flaws may be caused by ink crusts or foreign matter on the printing plate or cylinder, or by a fold or crease in the paper, and are therefore frequently transient. When a flaw is constant, that is, repeated throughout the part or whole of an issue, it may be termed a **variety**.

Flag Cancels (USA and Canada)

Ring flaw on Queen's neck

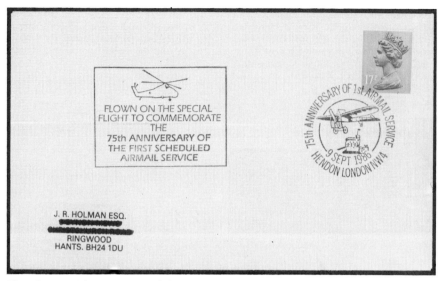

Flown Cover—carried on commemorative flight, 1986

Foreign Mail Stamps (Haiti, Turkey, Guatemala)

FLOWN COVER. A cover bearing evidence that it has been carried by airmail.

FLUORESCENCE. The emission of electromagnetic radiation, usually as visible light, as a result of the simultaneous absorption of radiation of shorter wavelength. Some printing inks used for stamps fluoresce in different colours when viewed by ultra-violet light, and some give off a brilliant glow. These characteristics are useful in the detection of repairs and other forms of fakes . In recent years optical brightening agents have been added to paper to improve the appearance of stamps. Such stamps may glow an intense whitish-violet when activated by either short- or long-wave ultra-violet light. These papers are referred to by such trade terms as "hi-brite" or "lo-brite". British Machin definitives were initially printed on original coated paper (OCP) but late in 1971 the printers introduced fluorescent coated paper (FCP) which gives a clearer impression. It is much whiter and reacts clearly under an ultra-violet lamp. Fluorescent security markings were introduced by the Cook Islands in 1968 and Ecuador in 1969. Those used by the Cook Islands are visible to the naked eye and take the form of an overall pattern of tiny coats of arms. ■

FOIL STAMPS. Stamps printed on paper faced with metal foil. Hungary pioneered this in 1955, when aluminium foil was used for a 5ft stamp commemorating the Light Metal Industries Congress. Metal foil was subsequently used by the USSR (1961), Tonga (1963) and many other countries, especially in 1969–70 when this fashion reached its zenith. Firms specialising in this technique included Walsall Security Printers (England), and Boccard and Marrotte (both France). ■

FOREIGN MAIL STAMPS. Stamps issued by several countries specifically for use on mail going overseas, and denoted either by the inscription or by the use of currency differing from the debased money used internally. Turkey pioneered this practice in 1901, with separate sets for inland and foreign mail, mainly printed matter. Haiti issued stamps (1906–19) for overseas mail denominated in "strong" currency (piastres) instead of the local currency (gourdes). Both Guatemala (1931–45) and Chile (1934–52) issued separate sets of airmail stamps for foreign and inland mail. *See also* Porte de Mar Stamps.

Forerunners (Jewish National Fund)

Fractional Currency—US paper money reproducing 5c. stamp (1862–76)

Frama Labels—British issue in use 1 May 1984–30 April 1985

Frame—GB 1929 ½d., King's portrait within oval frame, stamp design set within rectangular lined frame

FORERUNNERS. Stamps or labels, many of them **provisional** in nature, used before authorised issues are made for public use. The labels of the Jewish National Fund, for example, are regarded as forerunners of Israeli stamps, while the Sinn Fein labels are regarded as forerunners of the stamps of Ireland. Sometimes stamps of one country are used in another prior to the latter issuing its own, and these stamps with identifiable postmarks would also be regarded as forerunners, e.g. GB used in many colonies, Sarawak used in Brunei till 1907, or NZ used in Pitcairn till 1940.

FORGERY. An imitation of a stamp intended to deceive. Such stamps intended to defraud a postal administration are called postal forgeries, but the majority of forgeries were designed to deceive collectors. Genuine stamps with forged postmarks or overprints also come into this category. ■

FRACTIONAL CURRENCY. Form of paper money issued by the United States between 1862 and 1876 and reproducing postage stamps, a logical extension of the concept permitting stamps to circulate as legal tender currency during a shortage of coins.

FRACTIONAL STAMPS. Stamps cut into halves, thirds, quarters and even smaller fractions to denote a corresponding fraction of the original face value. The greatest variety was produced by Mexico between 1856 and 1866 when fractions as small as an eighth of the 8r denomination were employed.

FRAMA LABELS. A misnomer for postage stamps produced by micro-processor machines manufactured by the Frama company of Switzerland. These machines dispense a gummed stamp with a pre-printed design and a value determined by the coin or coins inserted by the customer, and the value selected by means of buttons. These stamps are more properly regarded as a form of **automatic stamp** although the British Post Office termed its own shortlived issue of 1984–5 **Royal Mail Postage Labels**.

FRAME. That part of the stamp which encloses the portrait, vignette or other motif.

FRANC DE DROITS. French expression meaning "free of dues", inscribed on labels used on overseas packets and parcels to secure delivery free of Customs duty, the charges being paid in advance by the sender. The FDD system, as it is known, is operated by most countries through the Universal Postal Union, using distinctive labels, usually in shades of yellow or orange, inscribed in French and often having the equivalent in the local language.

FRANCHISE STAMPS. Sometimes referred to as private stamps, they are usually issued to charitable or national institutions to permit mail bearing these stamps to pass through the mails free of postage. Stamps of this type have been issued by Portugal, Spain and Switzerland. Similar stamps are sometimes issued for use by military personnel, and this type has been issued by Germany, France, Italy and Vietnam.

FRANK. A mark or stamp on a piece of mail to indicate transmission without charge. Between 1653 and 1840 a franking privilege was enjoyed by Members of Parliament, the Royal Family and certain government officials who endorsed their mail by signature. Abuse of this privilege led to various measures to tighten up the regulations, including addressing in the same handwriting as the signature, and posting on the endorsed date. The franking privilege was abolished in 1840, and replaced by a system of exempting official correspondence by **certifying stamp**.

Franc de Droits— Customs charges paid in advance by sender

Franchise Stamps— Portuguese issue allowing free postage

Franc—1861 cover signed by Lord Campbell, transmitted free of postage

ON SERVICE

Free Xmas
Concession to
New Zealand only.

LONDON

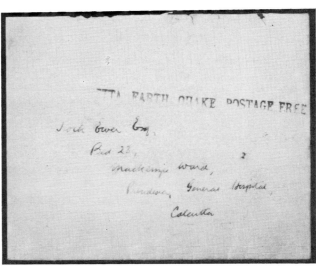

RECEIVED FROM H.M.SHIP.
NO CHARGE TO BE RAISED

RECEIVED FROM H.M. SHIP
NO CHARGE TO BE RAISED

JUN 11 17D

Free Mail—GB label and markings

FREE.

Date Stamp.

No Charge to be
made on Delivery.

Free Mail

FREE MAIL. Correspondence transmitted free of charge. In addition to letters sent under the franking privilege, noted above, this includes certain categories of forces' mail in wartime which may be found with postmarks inscribed POSTAGE FREE or RECEIVED FROM HM SHIPS – NO CHARGE TO BE ADDED. Other categories of mail transmitted free have included letters from and to Prisoners of War, and mail from disaster areas (e.g. the Quetta earthquake, India in June 1935).

FRESH ENTRY. The substitution of a new entry on an engraved plate for an unsatisfactory or defective original which has been erased. Sometimes vestiges of the first entry can result in a partial double impression.

FUGITIVE INKS. Inks containing chemicals or aqueous solvents which will change, fade or wash out if any attempt is made to tamper with the stamp (e.g. cleaning off the cancellation). De La Rue pioneered their single and double fugitive inks in the 1850s as a security device, notably the shades of green and purple. Vermilion (mercuric sulphide) was added to red pigments for the same purpose. Such stamps present problems for collectors, as they have to be handled with great care, especially in floating them off their backing paper. ■

German Type—overprint for use at German post offices in China

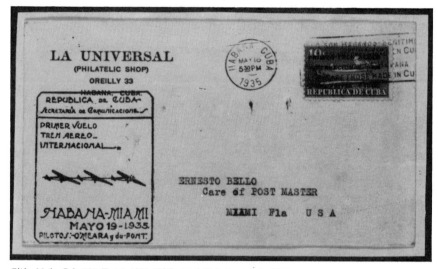

Glider Mail—Cuba 'Air Train', 1935; 'Glider Mail Flights' postmark, 1974

GERMAN TYPE. A form of printer's type characterised by heavy, angular and elaborate lettering, also known as "Gothic" or "Old English".

GLAZED PAPER. A highly-calendered paper without any special coating, sometimes confused with **enamelled paper** because of its considerable gloss. ∎

GLIDER MAIL. Mail conveyed by glider dates from 1923 when cards and covers were carried by gliders at an aviation meeting in Gersfeld, Germany, obsolete stamps of the 1919 series being overprinted for the occasion. Motor-assisted gliders conveyed mail from Lympne to Hastingleigh, England later the same year, and special labels were produced. The first international glider mail was flown from Graz, Austria to Maribor, Yugoslavia in 1933. Mail carried by strings of gliders towed by a powered aeroplane, known as the Lustig Sky

Train, was staged in the USA (1934), and a similar service operated in 1935 in Cuba, which issued a 10c stamp for the purpose.

GOLDBEATER'S SKIN. A thin, tough, translucent, resin-impregnated paper used for the 1886 parcel stamps of Germany. They were printed on a collodion surface on the reverse side, the gum being applied on top of the printing. These high-value stamps were not sold to the public, but affixed to parcels by counter clerks. **Pen-cancellation** was used as the most effective way of preventing the stamps ever being re-used. ∎

GRAND CONSOMMATION. Trade name (otherwise known as G.C.) for a pale grey granite paper of inferior quality, used for the printing of French stamps in the First World War during a shortage of the normal paper. ∎

GRANITE PAPER. A colloquial term for paper having coloured cotton, linen, jute or wool fibres embodied within it (in appearance, like the "veins" in granite), the fibres being introduced in the pulp stage of manufacture. It was used for the early stamps of Austria, Switzerland and other European countries, but has also been used for many photogravure stamps of Switzerland and Taiwan in more recent years. A paper of similar character, known as silk paper, was used for US revenue stamps. ■

GRAPHITE LINES. Vertical black lines printed on the back of certain British stamps in 1957. The substance used was called Naphthadag (Deflocculated Acheson's Graphite) and was employed in connexion with early experiments at Southampton with the automatic sorting of mail. Stamps intended for use on fully paid mail, such as sealed letters (and later first class mail) had two lines on the back, whereas the stamp intended to prepay the basic printed matter rate (and later the second class rate), had only one line. This permitted the segregation of mail into the basic categories for sorting and stamping. These lines were superseded by phosphor bands.

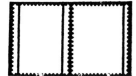

Graphite Lines—used on British stamps 1957–9 (one line on 2d.)

Greetings Stamp—Grenadines of Grenada, Easter 1976

GREETINGS LABELS, STAMPS AND STATIONERY. Christmas seals, stamps and aerogrammes are the best-known items in this category; but special covers and cards as well as adhesive stamps were produced by several German local posts in the late-19th century for New Year's greetings. Stamps for the Jewish New Year are regularly issued by Israel, while Manchuria, Japan, China, Hong Kong and other Far Eastern countries have celebrated the Lunar New Year in this manner. In recent years several countries have issued stamps for Easter, while the USA and Ireland have issued Love stamps for St Valentine's Day. Ireland also issues postal stationery for St Patrick's Day. The USA and some Latin American countries have issued stamps for Mothers' Day.

GRILLE. A security device in the form of small square dots embossed on certain stamps of the United States and Peru. These grilles, applied in square or diamond patterns, break up the paper fibres and allow the obliterating ink to penetrate more effectively and prevent any attempts to clean a stamp for re-use. ■

GUERRILLA STAMPS. Stamps issued by guerrilla forces date from 1895, when the underground fighters of Taiwan founded the Black Flag Republic to fight the Japanese occupying forces and issued stamps in connexion with their clandestine postal service. Later issues include the KKK stamps of the Aguinaldo partisans in the Philippines (1898), the Boer Commando issues in the South African War (1899–1902), the IRA stamps used in Co. Cork during the Irish Civil War (1922–3), the prolific issues of the Communist partisans in China from 1929 onwards and the stamps of the National Front for the Liberation of South Vietnam (1963–76).

Guerrilla Stamp (Philippines, 1898)

GUIDE LINES AND DOTS. Fine lines or dots marked upon the plate as a guide for the engraver or workman when transferring impressions. Normally these are removed after laying down the plate, but they are sometimes still visible on unprinted portions of the design, or in the stamp's margin.

Guide Lines and Dots—guide dot centrally placed above top frame line

Gutter—narrow (2½mm) and wide (3½mm)

*Gutter—GB commemorative stamps
in plain and 'traffic light' gutter pairs*

GUM. The adhesive substance usually found on the back of stamps when sold to the public. In this state they are described as having "full O.G." (original gum). A "regummed" stamp has had fresh gum added to convey the impression that it is O.G., and is therefore regarded as a form of **fake**. The gum used for the first British stamps was made of potato-starch, wheat-starch and acacia gum and officially known as "cement", according to the instructions for use, printed in the sheet margins of stamps. Green-tinted gum was used for the 6d embossed stamp of 1854, to enable the printer to distinguish the right side of the paper for printing. Red gum was used by Hanover (1850–9) for the same reason. Gum arabic was widely used till 1968 when invisible, non-curl PVA (polyvinyl alcohol) gum was introduced in Britain and subsequently extended to many other countries. Dextrin was added to the gum in 1973 (known as PVAD) and a bluish green colouring matter was then added to distinguish it from the earlier pure PVA gum. *See also* Economy Gum and Self-Adhesive Stamps and Labels. ■

GUM DEVICE. An imitation watermark on the gummed side of stamps. A pattern of wavy lines appeared in the gum of German stamps (1921), while a geometric device was employed in the stamps of Germany (1934), Switzerland and Liechtenstein (1936–9). Czech stamps of 1923 had the gum applied in a pattern showing the initials of the republic (CSP). ■

GUTTER. The space left between stamps to allow them to be separated or perforated. An interpane gutter is the blank space, usually of stamp format, between the panes of a sheet of stamps. This was a feature of some British letterpress stamps of the late 19th century. Gutters were re-introduced for British commemoratives in 1973, encouraging a fashion for collecting stamps in "gutter pairs".

HAIR LINES. Diagonal white lines which cross the outer corners of stamps printed from the reserve plates made by De La Rue in 1863 and designed to identify these plates. Only the 4d (plate 4), 6d (plate 4) and 9d (plate 3) were actually used to print stamps, the lastnamed being regarded as an **abnormal**. The term is also loosely used to describe fine scratches on a printing plate or cylinder resulting in colourless blemishes.

Hair Lines—GB 4d. with hair lines in each corner

HALF-TONE PROCESS. A photo-mechanical method of representing light and shade by dots of varying size, extensively used for the reproduction of illustration blocks in newspapers and magazines. Akin to photogravure in that the subject is photographed through a fine screen on a sensitised plate of copper or zinc and subsequently etched. Probably the cheapest reproductive medium and, for that reason, occasionally used in stamp printing. Examples include stamps of Kishangarh, Latvia, Saudi Arabia, Iran and the Netherlands.

HAND-MADE PAPER. Paper made by hand in moulds, and thus in separate sheets instead of machine-made continuous reels. The sheets are usually deckle-edged, i.e. rough or untrimmed, due to the uneven deckle or frame of the mould, or the wire-gauge sieve within it. The production of hand-made paper reflects the skill of the craftsman, and there is often considerable variation in thickness, even within the same sheet. ■

HAND-PAINTED. Colour applied to a stamp by hand after printing. Almost unknown in modern times, but a fairly common practice in the 19th century. This may range from the retouching of bicoloured stamps to correct faulty registration between the colours (e.g. the German high values of 1900), to the complete hand-painting of the Colombian tricolour flag on the **cubiertas** of 1865–70. ■

HANDSTAMP. Strictly speaking, the implement used to apply a postmark by hand, but often used loosely to signify the postmark itself. Many overprints and control marks were applied by means of handstamps.

HANDSTRUCK POSTAGE STAMPS. Marks made by handstamp direct on to postal packets to denote the prepayment of postage. The earliest of these stamps were those used by William **Dockwra** in his London Penny Post. Any "postage paid" postmark applied by hand comes into this category, although it tends to be confined to those antedating the advent of adhesive stamps. Many of these, however, were themselves produced in the 19th century by means of handstruck implements, e.g. the Afghan issues of 1882–90, the Bermuda "postmasters" issues of 1848–61, the Falkland Islands "Franks" (1861–77), and many issues from the Indian feudatory states, some American **carriers' stamps** and many of the provisional local issues from the Southern states during the American Civil War (1861–5).

Handstruck Postage Stamps—early issue of Indore and Bermuda

HARROW PERFORATION. A means of perforating whole sheets at a single stroke, the pins being arranged crosswise, rather like a honeycomb.

Harrow Perforation (Austria, perf 10½ harrow)

HEALTH STAMPS. Stamps bearing a charity premium specifically in aid of health camps and TB sanatoria for children. These stamps have been issued annually by New Zealand since 1929. Fiji issued them in 1951 and 1954 only.

Health Stamps

HELECON. A chemical substance of the zinc sulphide group added to the printing ink, or impregnated in the surface coating of stamps, to facilitate electronic sorting and segregation of mail. Helecon was first used for Australia's 11d (Bandicoot) stamp in 1963 and was subsequently employed in many definitives (sheets, coils and booklets) as well as commemoratives. During 1964–5 many stamps were issued on both Helecon and ordinary paper, but since 1966 all Australian stamps have been printed on Helecon paper or paper coated with a similar luminescent substance. ■

HELICOPTER MAIL. Mail carried by rotary wing aircraft. The first mail in this category was flown by autogiro at the APEX exhibition, London in 1934. The first helicopter mail service operated in Los Angeles in 1946. This medium spread to Europe in 1947 (Hague-Brussels service) and England in 1948 (East Anglia). This medium is widely used nowadays for airmail "feeder" services, and also the supply of offshore oil-rigs and other places where landing by conventional fixed-wing aircraft would be difficult. Distinctive covers and cachets have been used in this connexion.

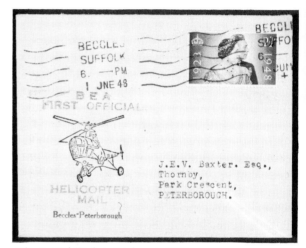

Helicopter Mail (Beccles to Peterborough, 1948)

HIDDEN DATES. Canadian stamps since 1935 incorporate the date of manufacture in minuscule numerals, usually concealed somewhere in the design.

Canadian stamp showing location of hidden date (1986)

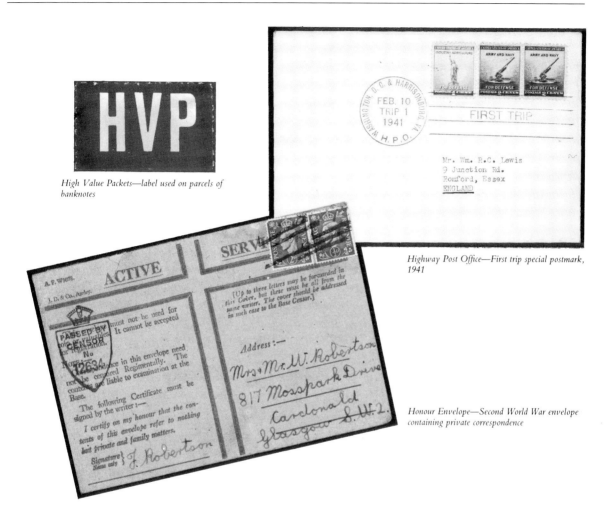

High Value Packets—label used on parcels of banknotes

Highway Post Office—First trip special postmark, 1941

Honour Envelope—Second World War envelope containing private correspondence

HIGH VALUE PACKETS. Parcels of banknotes and high-security documents, transmitted by the British Post Office on behalf of the clearing banks, 1930–73, and distinguished by red labels inscribed HVP.

HIGHWAY POST OFFICE. Motor vehicle used in the United States to operate a postal service in rural areas, picking up, sorting and dropping mail en route. The service was inaugurated in 1941 and used postmarks inscribed H.P.O. Similar services using distinctive handstamps are now in operation in other countries.

HOLED. Stamps which have been pierced with holes, a distressingly common feature of British line-engraved stamps,

due to the fashion in the 1840s and 1850s for piercing them with a needle and threading them together to form "snakes". The term is also applied to stamps with a hole punched out of them, a common form of cancelling stamps used telegraphically.

HONOUR ENVELOPE. Manilla envelope bearing a cross and inscription in green, signifying its use by forces on active service who certified on their honour that the contents did not discuss military matters. The use of these envelopes during the Second World War obviated the necessity to censor forces' mail at regimental level and thus preserved a measure of privacy - although these honour envelopes were liable to examination by the base censor.

HOODED DATESTAMP. A circular datestamp having an additional concentric segment around the top in the form of a hood, for the purpose of containing a distinctive inscription. Stamps of this type are used to this day in Britain for registration and confirmation of telegrams, but they were also employed for certain special purposes in the late 19th century (e.g. Late Fee postings, mail from the Royal Household, overseas correspondence of government departments, etc) and were also issued to certain Irish offices for ordinary use - Cork, Waterford, Londonderry and Limerick (hence the term "Cowall" cancellations used by Irish collectors).

Hooded Datestamps—mostly used for registered mail

HOTEL POSTS. Stamps were issued in connexion with services organised by hotels in remote areas, to convey guests' mail to the nearest post office. These stamps were issued by many hotels in Switzerland (1864–99), in the Carpathian districts of Hungary and Rumania (1895–1926) and in Austria (1927–38). Many post offices throughout the world have, or had, their own post offices and mail bearing their distinctive postmarks is now much sought after.

Hotel Post stamps

Hyphen Perforation—GB insured labels

HYPHEN PERFORATION. Sometimes referred to as "hyphen-hole", this is a form of perforation in which the paper is punched out in long, narrow strips instead of the usual round discs. As such, it is often confused with straight-line **roulette** but differs from that in that the paper is punched out and not merely pierced. Sometimes referred to as "slot perforation", it is commonly used in Britain for many kinds of postal labels.

IMITATION PERFORATION. Simulated denticulation printed round stamps. The first issue of Sirmoor, when reprinted in 1891, was copied, with perforations, from a dealer's catalogue. Stamps of Obock (1893–4) and Djibouti (1894–1902) were issued imperforate, but had imitation perforations as a border decoration. This has also been a feature of some South African **Christmas seals** in recent years.

IMITATION STAMPS. Postal administrations have been known to produce imitations of their own stamps, when the original plates are no longer available for **reprints.** These official imitations may differ from the originals in paper, gum, size, colour and design detail. They are known to have been produced to fill gaps in official collections and exhibitions, as well as for sale to collectors.

IMPERFORATE. Without perforation or other means of separation, and therefore requiring to be cut apart by means of a knife or scissors. The British line-engraved stamps of 1840–54, the embossed stamps of 1847–54, and the early issues of many other countries, were imperforate. **Frama labels** are also imperforate, as they are issued singly from machines. The term is often shortened to "Imperf". Stamps without perforations on one or more sides (e.g. from coils or booklets) may be described as "partially perforated".

Imitation Perforation (Djibouti, 1894–1902)

Imitation Stamp—official and imitation stamps of Persia (note difference in size)

IMPERFORATE BETWEEN. Stamps normally perforated, but with a line of perforations inadvertently omitted between adjoining rows, due to faulty manufacture. Can apply to horizontal or vertical rows.

IMPERIAL REPLY COUPONS. *See* International Reply Coupons.

IMPRESSED WATERMARK. An imitation watermark impressed on the stamp by die-stamping. Swiss stamps of the 1862 issue had such a device, consisting of a cross within an oval, embossed on the back.

IMPRIMATUR. Latin word meaning "Let it be printed", applied philatelically to the first sheet printed from an approved and finished printing plate, or stamps from such a sheet. It was the custom for British printers to produce six sheets, one of which was retained as the Imprimatur, while the other five were gummed and perforated and put into circulation. Sometimes plates were not put to press in the normal way, and the stamps from these five sheets are classed as **Abnormals.** ■

Imperforate Between (Surinam, Mexico)

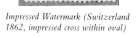

Impressed Watermark (Switzerland 1862, impressed cross within oval)

Imprints—on stamp (Malagasy) and in sheet margin

Inland Mail Stamps—(Madagascar, 1895; Liberia, 1897)

IMPRINT. The name of the printer or issuing authority inscribed on the sheet margins, or on the stamps themselves. In the latter case the names of the designer and engraver are sometimes included below the foot of the stamp design.

INDIA-PAPER. A thin, soft, absorbent paper, of Chinese or Japanese origin (made from bamboo fibre), used in taking the finest proofs from engraved plates; also a thin, tough, opaque paper used for the compact printing of voluminous texts, such as the Bible, but also used occasionally for stamp proofs. ■

INK. Mixture of pigments, oils, varnishes, driers, toners, wax compounds and fugitive chemicals, concocted in accordance with the type of printing process, the kind of press and the thickness and quality of paper to be used. For example, the ink used in the **intaglio** method is almost solid and has to be daubed and squeezed into the recesses on the plate, whereas the inks used in lithography or letterpress are far less viscous. Over-inking can cause heavy, smudged impressions, while under-inking produces a thin impression. Faulty adjustment of the knife, used to wipe excess ink off rotary printing cylinders, produces **Doctor Blade flaws.** Faulty inking in general may result in blotches, blemishes, white or coloured patches and streaking on the stamps. ■

INLAND MAIL STAMPS. Stamps intended specifically for internal mail and thus inscribed. The British consular mail in Madagascar (1895), as well as Liberia (1897), issued stamps designated in this way.

INSERTED BY HAND. A minor type of **hand-painting** in which missing letters, accents, etc., usually in typeset overprints, have been touched in on the stamp manually.

Inserted by Hand (Ireland, 1922—accent inserted)

FRAGILE

The extra fee paid on this parcel is to ensure special handling during transmission through the post.

P.P.9

POSTES-CANADA-POST

PERISHABLE

PÉRISSABLE

33-86-105 (5-72)

INSTRUCTIONAL LABELS AND MARKS. These are widely used by postal authorities to indicate special handling of mail in transit. In this category come those labels inscribed "Fragile", "Perishable", "First Class", "Letter", "Urgent", "Small Packet" or their equivalents in other languages. Some countries even have labels to denote philatelic mail, to ensure clear postmarking and careful handling. *See also* Charge, Directional and Explanatory Marks; Philatelic Handling Labels.

INSURED MAIL. Letters, packets and parcels insured against loss on the payment of a special fee by the sender. Prior to 1878 no compensation was granted by the British Post Office for loss or damage, but thereafter a small sum became payable in respect of registered items. This was extended in 1886, when a fee of 2d would insure against loss up to £10. This scheme was subsequently expanded, particularly in respect of overseas parcels for which registration was not always available. The Universal Postal Union introduced special red labels, inscribed VALEUR DÉCLARÉE, and these have been used in many different variants by member countries. Some countries also use special types of **registration label** for this purpose, either printed in different colours, or having the letter V substituted for R in the left-hand panel.

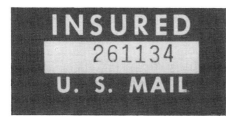

INTAGLIO. Italian word (pronounced "intalyo") meaning "in recess", originally employed to describe the technique of recess engraving precious stones used as seals, but later extended to cover the printing process alternatively known as line-engraving or recess-printing. It should be noted, however, that **photogravure** is a photo-mechanical version of intaglio, as it operates on the same principle. In this process the ink lies in the recesses and the paper is forced into them to take up the ink, hence the characteristic grooves and ridges on stamps printed by this method.

INTELPOST. Electronic facsimile system for the transmission of documents, used by several postal administrations, including the British. Following transmission, the documents are either collected from the office of reception, or put into the post for delivery in the normal way. Special labels, postmarks and stationery have been produced in connexion with this service.

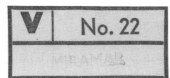

Insured Mail—Valeur Declaree labels

Intelpost—envelope used by British Post Office

INTERMEDIATE PERFORATION. A term applied specifically to Perkins Bacon printings of the 1860s, in which perforations produced by a certain machine deteriorated from the original clean-cut to intermediate and finally rough.

INTERNATIONAL REPLY COUPON. Sometimes abbreviated to IRC, these are slips issued by member-countries of the Universal Postal Union to provide a convenient method of sending reply postage with letters going overseas. The coupons are readily exchanged at any post office for postage stamps equivalent to the surface postage on mail going abroad. These coupons were introduced in 1908 and over the intervening years their design has been greatly simplified. Originally coupons bore the name of the issuing country, but later only the denomination in local currency was expressed. Now even that distinction has disappeared and IRCs are identical the world over, apart from the postmark of the issuing office. The same concept was at one time used for Imperial or Commonwealth Reply Coupons, used by Britain and the overseas dominions and colonies.

Intermediate Perforation (St. Vincent, 1861)

International Reply Coupon— British Commonwealth and Imperial versions (now superseded by the single-purpose IRC)

INTERNEE MAIL. Correspondence from persons interned during time of war. Special labels were provided for the free transmission of letters from French troops interned in Switzerland during the Franco-German War (1870–1). Distinctive postmarks were used in both World Wars on mail from enemy aliens interned in the Isle of Man. Special stamps are known to have been used at Ruhleben (Germany), Bando (Japan) and Knockaloe (Isle of Man) on internees' inter-camp mail. Distinctive **censor marks** were used in Northern Ireland during the period when internment was in force. *See also* Concentration Camp and Prisoner of War Mail.

Internee Mail—Gratis label for use on prisoner's mail

Interpostal Seal—Egyptian interpostal (Jaffa)

INTERPOSTAL SEALS. Circular adhesive labels serving two purposes: to seal the flaps of envelopes, and to signify official correspondence entitled to transmission through the post free of charge. A wide range of these seals, with the names of various post offices, was used on official mail of the Egyptian Post Office. Similar seals have been used by the German states, Austria and the Netherlands along the same lines as **certifying stamps** in Britain.

INTER-PROVINCIALS. Stamps issued by colonies or provinces which later become federated, with a unified postal service permitting the use of each territory's stamps in the other territories of the union. The term arose in 1910, when stamps of the Cape of Good Hope, Natal, the Orange River Colony and the Transvaal were permitted to be used anywhere within the Union of South Africa, pending the introduction of the Union's own stamps. It would also be applicable to the usage of the stamps of the Australian states, after the establishment of the Australian Commonwealth in 1902, and analogous to the use of stamps of Tanzania, Kenya or Uganda in each other, during the period when their posts were unified under the East African Posts and Telecommunications Corporation.

INTERRUPTED PERFORATION. A means of strengthening strips of stamps used in automatic vending machines, where gaps are created in the line of perforations by the omission of certain pins. This device was used by Danzig and the Netherlands.

INVALIDATED. A stamp which is no longer valid for the prepayment of postage. *See also* Demonetised.

Interrupted Perforation (Netherlands, Danzig)

INVERTED CENTRE. A stamp in which the central vignette is upside down in relation to the frame. Such an error arises when two-colour stamps are being printed and the sheets are fed into the press a second time the wrong way up.

Inverted Centre (Dominican Republic)

INVERTED FRAME. A stamp in which the frame is upside down in relation to the centre. It has now been proved that the so-called Inverted Swan of Western Australia came into this category, as the error was caused by inversion of the lithographic transfer for the frame of one stamp in the sheet. Brazil's 100 reis of 1891 is another example of an inverted frame.

Inverted Frame (Western Australia)

Inverted Overprint—GB GOVT. PARCELS

INVERTED OVERPRINT. A stamp whose overprint is upside down in relation to the stamp itself, caused by inserting sheets of stamps into the overprinting press the wrong way up.

INVERTED WATERMARK. Watermark upside down in relation to the image on the stamp. This happened frequently when sheets of stamps were printed one at a time. It also occurs in modern reel-fed stamps printed for booklet panes. As they were arranged alternatively upside down to facilitate separation by guillotine, it follows that 50 per cent of the panes from booklets would have upright and the rest inverted watermarks.

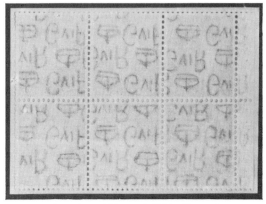

above *Inverted Watermark (GB booklet pane)*
below *Irregular Perforation (Mexico)*

IRREGULAR PERFORATION. Perforations out of alignment, or of mixed gauge in one or more lines or sides of the same stamp.

ITALIC LETTERING. A fount of type in which the letters slope upwards towards the right. In typography italics are normally used for emphasis, but in stamps and overprints italic lettering is merely employed for decorative effect.

IVORY HEAD. Nickname for British stamps of 1841–57 to which prussiate of potash had been added to the ink as a security feature. This produced a blue effect at its densest where the printing was heaviest on the face of the stamp. When viewed from the back the blue effect was diffused through the paper, but being lightest in the area of the Queen's profile it created an effect like an ivory cameo.   ■

JAPANESE PAPER. Also known as native paper, this was a soft, fine paper made from the bark of the mulberry tree, the long fibres accounting for its renowned strength. It may be found in varying degrees of texture and thickness, either wove or laid, and was used for printing the early issues of Japan.   ■

JOINED PAPER. Paper with a slight overlap where two strips of stamps from a sheet have been joined at the **selvage** to form a continuous coil. This may be found on certain coil stamps which are collected in coil-join pairs. The term is also applied to paper in reels joined for continuous printing. Stamps on paper from the junction of the reels may be much thicker than normal as a result.

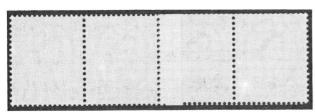

Joined Paper (GB 4d. Wilding)

JOINT LINE. The coloured line that often appears between coil stamps where the curved plates on a rotary press meet. The microscopic line between the plate ends picks up sufficient ink to print a line resembling a guide line in the colour of the stamps.

Joint Line (USA Consumer Education stamp)

JOURNAL TAX STAMPS. Stamps denoting taxes on newspapers, but often conferring free transmission through the post. The red stamps impressed on the front pages of British newspapers would come into this category, but the term is applied specifically to certain adhesive stamps of France and Austria.

Impressed Newspaper Tax Stamp (Ireland)   *Journal Tax Stamp (France, 1868)*

JUBILEE LINE. A line of marginal rule, either continuous or co-extensive (broken into lengths equal to each stamp) found in the **selvage** of British stamps. It derives its name from the fact that it was first used in the 1887 definitive series, issued in the year of Queen Victoria's Golden Jubilee. The line, in the form of thin brass strip, relieved the pressure on the printing plates in the marginal areas. It was also a feature of many colonial stamps, produced by the letterpress or photogravure methods, and is now more properly termed a "marginal rule".

Jubilee Line (British Honduras Victorian issue, with plate number 2)

KEY PLATE. The plate which prints the general design on stamps, specifically certain British Commonwealth issues, requiring two separate printings, used in conjunction with a separate and variable **Duty Plate**. Also known as the Head plate as it usually bears the head of the reigning sovereign.

Key Plate (Duty plate section obliterated)

KEY TYPE. Term for uniform designs used in the stamps of many colonial empires of the 19th and early 20th centuries. The idea was originated by Perkins Bacon who printed stamps for Mauritius, Barbados and Trinidad in 1848–54 using a standard Britannia design. De La Rue refined the concept in 1879 with letterpress designs using a standard key plate and variable duty plates bearing the names of the different colonies. Colonial key types survived in the Leeward Islands, as late as 1956. Spain and Portugal adopted the "Britannia" principle in 1855 and 1870 respectively, but Portugal subsequently adopted the key type principle in 1897. France (1892–1908) and Germany (1900–14) made extensive use of this system, while Belgium, the Netherlands and Denmark preferred uniform designs rather than standard key plates.

Key Type (Leeward Islands—same design used 1890–1956)

Killer postmark on GB stamp

KILLER. Nickname for an obliteration that effectively "kills" a stamp and prevents re-use. Most killers belong to the 19th century, when postal administrations were particularly obsessed by the fear of re-used stamps, and take the form of heavy bars (UK), grids (France) or the distinctive **cork cancels** of Canada and the USA.

KILOWARE. Used stamps on piece, culled by postal administrations from parcel cards and sold to dealers and collectors by the kilo. The term is also loosely applied to any stamps used on paper and sold by weight, but collected by banks, missions and charities.

KOCHER STAMPS. A. Kocher et Fils of La Chaux de Fonds and Vevey, Switzerland took advantage of a loophole in the Swiss postal regulations (which permitted private stationery stamped to order) to have impressions of the "Tell's Son" definitives in 1909 on the firm's adhesive labels, the stamps being framed by advertising matter. After some 16,000 had been printed the Swiss authorities withdrew the privilege and these "framed stamps" or "stamps on a sticker" became obsolete.

LABELLED STAMPS. Stamps with labels attached, either as **advertising labels**, or as decorative or commemorative **coupons**. Italian stamps were issued for wartime propaganda purposes, with pictorial labels alongside and as an integral part of the stamp. Stamps of Belgium, Germany and Hungary have been issued with integral labels at the foot giving details of the reason for a charity premium. Belgian stamps with detachable **Dominical labels** were issued in connexion with Sunday delivery. Stamps of the Mexican state of Sonora were printed with labels denoting fiscal usage, to be removed if the stamps were intended for postal use.

LABELS. Slips of paper, usually with an adhesive backing. Technically speaking adhesive postage stamps are labels, and they were thus described by the British Post Office when introduced in 1840, but collectors now tend to make a distinction between stamps, which have postal validity, and anything else which has not. Occasionally terminology becomes confused, as in the expressions **"Frama labels"** and **"Royal Mail postage labels"**, both of which are postage stamps. Labels may be produced by non-postal bodies for commemorative, advertising or charitable purposes, while postal labels range from airmail **etiquettes** to **charge**, **directional**, **explanatory** and **instructional labels**. Other postal categories include seals and sealing labels and testing labels for vending machines.

LAID PAPER. Paper which shows a pattern of watermarked lines set closely together, the lines being caused by the parallel wires forming the base of the mould, or covering the dandyroll in machine-made paper, and usually crossed by widely-spaced lines. Described as "vertically laid" or "horizontally laid", according to the direction of the lines in relation to the design of the stamp.

Laid Paper

Late Fee Stamps (Colombia, Panama)

Labelled Stamps—Advertising (Belgium, Ireland, Italy, GB)

LATE FEE POSTMARKS AND STAMPS. These are employed to denote the payment of additional fees on correspondence put into the post after the normal hours of closure, in order to connect with evening despatches by mail trains. Postmarks inscribed TOO LATE, however, explained the apparent delay in transmission of mail, indicating that it had been held back till despatch the following morning. Postmarks used in connexion with the Late Fee system were often of a distinctive shape (e.g. the octagonal and hooded types used in Britain). Late fee stamps were issued by Colombia (1888–1914), Ecuador (1945), Panama (1903–16) and Uruguay (1936) and may usually be recognised by the word RETARDO. Victoria issued late fee stamps in 1855–7 and these were inscribed TOO LATE.

LECOCQ PRESS. A French machine which printed stamps for Peru in a continuous strip, the stamps being either cut up or issued in lengths after being rouletted.

LETTER CARD. Form of postal stationery consisting of cards folded over and sealed on the outer edges by perforated strips which can be removed by the recipient. It was pioneered by Belgium (1882), used privately in Britain (1887) and intro-

duced by the Post Office (1892). Newfoundland was the only country to issue reply letter cards (1912), with a smaller card inside. Letter cards have declined in popularity in recent years, and Britain discontinued then in the 1970s, preferring **post-notes** instead.

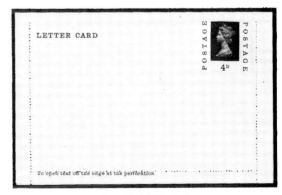

Letter Card (GB, 1968)

LETTER SHEET. Form of postal stationery consisting of a sheet of writing paper with some form of stamp denoting the prepayment of postage or exemption from charges. Pre-stamped letter sheets were pioneered by Sardinia (1818) and known as **Cavallini** from the tax device impressed on them. The first letter sheets bearing an impression signifying purely postal (as opposed to fiscal) charges were issued by New South Wales (1838). Letter sheets bearing a pictorial design by **Mulready** were issued in Britain at the same time as the Penny Black. Some countries, however, had more faith in such sheets and issued them before adhesive stamps, including Russia and Finland (1845), Thurn and Taxis (1846), Hanover (1849) and Poland (1858).

Sardinia 'Cavallini' letter sheet

LETTERPRESS. The correct term for the printing process sometimes referred to by philatelists as surface-printing or typography. It denotes printing from raised type, the actual image being in relief on the printing plate. The die is engraved so that the unwanted parts of the design are cut away. Duplicate impressions are electrotyped or stereotyped from the original die, and the resulting **cliches** are then assembled in a forme to make the printing plate. This process was used by De La Rue for fiscal stamps (from 1853) and postage stamps (from 1855). It continued to be used in Britain for postage stamps till 1934 and for **postage due labels** as late as 1971. It was actually first used for stamps in 1849 (both France and Bavaria) and was at one time the most popular printing process. Nowadays it tends to be confined to French low values and West German coil stamps. *See also* Typeset stamps. ∎

LIFE INSURANCE STAMPS. Postage stamps for use on mail by the Government Life Insurance Department have been issued by New Zealand since 1891. A stylised lighthouse provided the motif for the earlier issues, but between 1947 and 1981 pictorial designs featured famous lighthouses.

New Zealand Life Insurance Dept stamps

LINE BLOCK. An illustration block produced in a similar fashion to a half-tone, but without the screen. In printing from line blocks (in conjunction with letterpress), only extreme contrast is possible, though graduated tones may be suggested by the use of lines of varying thickness. ∎

LINE ENGRAVING. A method of engraving lines in recess on steel or copper to produce plates suitable for the **intaglio** process, otherwise known as *taille-douce*, copperplate or recess-printing. This technique is of great antiquity, and is similar to that employed in wax-resist etching. It was used in the production of banknotes and other forms of security printing from the 18th century onwards, and was adapted to stamp production by Perkins, Bacon and Petch for the world's first adhesive postage stamps in 1840. The design image is cut on a soft steel master die, in the correct size, in recess and reverse. The die is then hardened chemically and its image transferred to a soft steel cylinder, known as a transfer roller, under pressure. The roller in turn is chemically hardened and its image or images transferred to a soft steel plate, as many times as are required to build up the number of subjects to appear on the sheet of stamps. The process of transferring these images under pressure is known as rocking-in. The steel plate is then hardened and either remains flat (for flatbed printing) or is curved to fit a cylinder (rotary printing). At this stage the image on the plate is in reverse, so that the printed stamps will be the right way round. Ink is applied to the design recesses and the excess carefully wiped off and the surface of the plate polished before printing begins. The paper was at one time dampened prior to printing, in order to force it under pressure into the recesses and pick up the ink, but this is no longer necessary. Uneven shrinkage of the paper as it dried created problems when the first attempts were made to perforate stamps, and explains the poor centring of many British and colonial stamps produced by Perkins Bacon in the 1850s. These stamps are popularly known as Line-engraveds. ■

LINE PERFORATION. The simplest form of perforation in which rows of stamps are punched in single lines, the sheets then being turned sideways on to the perforator and the process repeated row by row. Line-perforated stamps can usually be identified by the fact that the intersecting holes at the corners of the stamps are never - or very rarely - precisely matched.

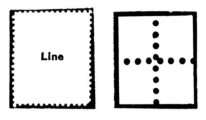

Corner intersections

LITERACY FUND STAMPS. Stamps issued by Haiti and Mexico for compulsory use at certain times of the year, the premiums being used in government campaigns to combat illiteracy. These stamps are inscribed "Alphabetisation" or "Alphabetizacion", in French and Spanish respectively.

Literacy Fund Stamps (Haiti)

LITHOGRAPHY. Printing process, from the Greek words *lithos* a stone, and *graphein*, to write. It was devised in 1795 by Alois Senefelder and derives its name from the use of polished limestone slabs, though nowadays zinc or even paper plates are used instead. The design is laid down on the stone or plate in greasy ink, or by means of transfers, in reverse. After fixing by acid, the stone is continually dampened in the course of

printing, but the printing ink only adheres to the greased image which repels the water. A printed image is obtained when paper is brought in contact with the inked stone. A modern variant of this is known as **offset lithography**. ■

LOCAL CARRIAGE LABELS. A term devised by the Philatelic Traders' Society in Britain to describe labels that purported to prepay the carriage on parcels and packets conveyed from certain offshore islands to the mainland. For some islands a regular local postal service is operated; but for others the service is irregular or non-existent. The labels are sometimes referred to as "British local issues". There was a rash of such issues in the 1960s and 1970s aimed mainly at the thematic market and collectors of special event material.

Local Carriage Label (Lundy, Bristol Channel, 1929)

LOCAL PROVISIONALS. Provisional stamps, surcharges, overprints or bisects prepared on the spot, during temporary shortages of certain denominations, under the authority of the local postmaster - as opposed to provisionals produced by the central postal authority for the same reason.

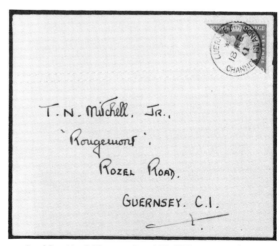

Local Provisional (Guernsey Second World War emergency bisect)

LOCAL STAMPS. Postage stamps whose validity and use are limited in area to a prescribed district, town or country, or on certain routes where there is no government postal service. They may be issued by private **carriers** and freight companies, municipal authorities or private individuals. *See also* Bypost, Christmas Charity Post Stamps, Circular Delivery, College Stamps, Hotel Posts, Local Carriage labels, Postmasters' stamps, Railway and Shipping Company stamps and Zemstvo stamps.

LOOSE LETTER. A letter, usually from an incoming ship, put into the post at the port of arrival, without a previous cancellation or postmark of origin. Special postmarks thus inscribed were applied to such mail at Australian seaports. *See also* Paquebot and Ship Letter.

LOTTERY STAMPS. Postage stamps issued by Norway in 1964 inscribed PORTO BETALT LYKKEBREVET (postage paid - chain letter). These stamps were sold for 2.50 kr. but had only 50 ore franking validity, the remaining 2 kr. being credited to a United Nations refugee fund. In addition, each stamp bore a serial number representing participation in a lottery which took place later that year.

LOVE STAMPS. Postage stamps issued primarily for use on greetings cards, exchanged by lovers on St Valentine's Day (14 February). The United States pioneered Love stamps in 1973 and repeated the experiment in 1982, 1984 and 1986. One of Britain's **Europa** stamps of 1981 celebrated St Valentine's Day, while Ireland has issued Love stamps since 1985.

Love Stamp (USA, 1982)

LOZENGE ROULETTE. *See* Diamond Roulette.

LUMINESCENCE. The light or glow emitted by a stamp when activated by either short- or long-wave ultra-violet light. Paper or ink containing a luminescent material has been used partly to brighten the appearance of stamps, but more specifically to assist automatic sorting and handling of mail. *See also* Fluorescence, Helecon Paper, Phosphor Bands and Tagged Stamps. ■

Lottery Stamp (Norway, 1964)

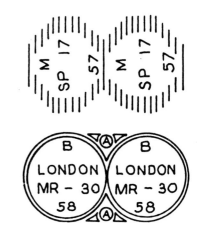

Machine Cancellation (GB early experimental cancels)

MACHINE CANCELLATION. The obliteration of postage stamps by mechanical means. The first attempt at machine cancellation was made in England in 1857, Pearson Hill having devised a machine for this purpose. Subsequently the British Post Office preferred the Pivot and Parallel Motion machines which were gadgets to assist manual stamping rather than machines in the true sense. It was left to Germany and the United States to develop automatic rapid-cancelling machines in the 1860s and 1870s. Both German and American single-impression machines were tested in England from 1885 onwards. Continuous-impression machines were pioneered by Krag of Norway. Cancelling machines usually have a dater die, showing the name of the office and the date of posting, and an obliterating element consisting of straight or wavy lines, or a **slogan**. Machines may also be fitted with Paid dies for the processing of bulk postings pre-paid in cash.

MAILOMAT. A system of **automatic stamps** used in Canada and the United States using Pitney Bowes postage **meters** adapted for use as coin-operated machines. They are installed in department stores, railway stations and the lobbies of post offices and provide the public with a form of postage stamp outside normal post office hours. These machines dispense gummed slips resembling **meter marks** but distinguished by the inclusion of the letters PO in the dater portion.

Mailomat (USA, Canada)

MALTESE CROSS. Strictly speaking, the distinctive eight-pointed cross used as the emblem of the Knights of St John of Malta and used frequently in both the stamps and machine cancellations of Malta, as well as the labels of the Sovereign Order of the Knights from their headquarters in Italy. It is the nickname given by philatelists to the obliterating device introduced in 1840 and intended to cancel the earliest British stamps.

These obliterators are, however, more likely to have been modelled on the Tudor rose emblem. They were superseded in 1844 by numeral obliterators. Distinctive crosses were used by a number of offices, usually when replacements were supplied after the initial issue. Originally red ink was used, changed to black in 1841, but other colours were occasionally employed.

Maltese Cross—numerous variations exist

MANILLA PAPER. A coarse, strong paper of light texture, originally manufactured from Manilla hemp, usually pale brown in colour and with one glazed side. Used in making envelopes and wrappers, a heavier gauge being used in some postcards. ∎

MANUSCRIPT OVERPRINT AND SURCHARGE. The alteration of a stamp's purpose, place of validity or face value by pen and ink. Such instances are relatively rare. Probably the best known case occurred in 1930 when Australian three-halfpenny Sturt commemoratives were overprinted P.M.L.H.I. by the Postmaster of Lord Howe Island and surcharged "2d Paid". Trinidad 6d stamps were surcharged in red ink (1882) to convert them to 1d stamps.

Manuscript Postmark (Gilbert & Ellice Is., 1944)

MANUSCRIPT POSTMARK. Many small post offices were not equipped with **datestamps** and the postmasters therefore had to insert the office name and date in manuscript in the space provided on parcel labels, registration receipts and other documents. This practice continued in Britain as late as 1904 when even the smallest offices were given **Climax daters**. It survived in many other parts of the world, notably the Pacific islands. **Pen-cancellation** of adhesive stamps and postal stationery has also been used in emergency. It is only of interest to the collector, however, if the practice was regular; the occasional obliteration of stamps which have missed cancellation, by ball-point pen, has no philatelic significance or value. Likewise, stamps cancelled in manuscript to denote fiscal usage have relatively little interest for philatelists.

MAP-BACKS. Stamps of Latvia issued in December 1918, and printed on the backs of German war maps, a portion of which may therefore be found on the back of each stamp.

MARGIN. The paper bordering the stamps in a sheet, as well as the blank paper bordering the printed image on the stamps themselves. *See also* Wing Margin.

MARGINAL ADVERTISING. Announcements of a postal or commercial nature, printed in the sheet margins of some stamps. This medium has been used by Germany, France, New Zealand and South Africa for commercial purposes, and by Great Britain and the United States for purely postal purposes.

MARGINAL GUIDE MARKS. Lines, dots, arrows and other marks in the margins of sheets of stamps, serving as a guide for the printer in perforating and trimming the sheets. *See also* Black Bar, Electric Eye Mark.

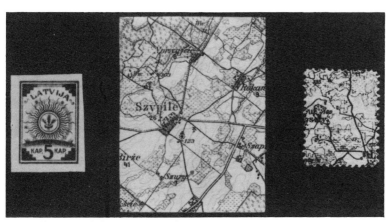

Map-Backs—Latvia, 1918—one map contained 228 stamps

Marginal Advertising—France—
Byrrh reconforte

Marginal Guide Marks
(Malta, intersecting lines)

Marginal Inscriptions (GB—total value of sheet of stamps)

Marginal Watermark (Turks Is., 1882, full inscription reads 'CROWN AGENTS FOR THE COLONIES')

Marine Insurance Stamp (Netherlands)

MARGINAL INSCRIPTIONS. Inscriptions in the sheet margins of stamps. They may include the name of the issuing authority, the printer's name, address and trademark, known as the **imprint**, **cylinder**, **plate** or **control numbers**, advertising matter, instructions for the use of the stamps, and the values of rows or the entire sheet.

MARGINAL WATERMARK. A watermark which is designed to appear only in the sheet margin, as opposed to that appearing on the stamps themselves. This may take the form of the name of the papermaker, the printer or the issuing authority.

MARINE INSURANCE STAMPS. Special stamps, inscribed "Drijvende Brandkast" (floating safe), issued by Holland and the Dutch East Indies in 1921 to prepay the fees payable on mail carried aboard ship in safes which were designed to float free, should the ship sink. This idea arose because of the great loss of shipping during the First World War due to submarine activity, and led the Universal Postal Union to promulgate a special tariff for this purpose in 1920. The service was very little used and was, in fact, formally abolished by the Universal Postal Union in 1924.

MARITIME MAIL. Mail brought ashore from warships and other naval vessels and therefore entitled to exemption from postal charges, or other form of preferential treatment. Special postmarks were used at British seaports in the First World War

Maritime Mail (Forces mail postmark, applied in London)

to signify that mail had been received from H.M. Ships and that no charge was to be raised. During the Second World War the term was changed to Maritime Mail to take account of the fact that mail from Allied shipping also qualified for this special treatment, and this term has continued to be used ever since.

MATCHED PAIR. A term usually applied to British Penny Blacks and Penny Reds printed from the same plates and bearing identical check letters. It has also been applied to any other pair of stamps which possess some common factor, e.g. British line-engraved stamps of 1854–60 with two different Scots local cancellations from the same office. ■

MAXIMUM CARD. A picture postcard bearing a postage stamp and postmark relevant to the picture on the card. The stamp and postmark are usually placed on the picture side to heighten the effect. This fashion began in Europe at the beginning of the 20th century and reached such a pitch that several countries, notably France and Germany, even had special explanatory marks applied to the address side to indicate that the postage stamps were on the other side. Maximaphily, as it is termed, gained enormously in popularity from the 1940s onwards, when many postal administrations began issuing First Day and special postmarks and latterly postcards either reproducing postage stamps, or featuring the pictures from which their motifs were derived. This branch of philately was hampered in Britian by PO regulations which were not relaxed until 1970. Since 1973, however, when the British PO began issuing PHQ cards, maximaphily has gained enormously in popularity.

Maximum Card (France, 1958)

Metal Currency Stamps (Peru, Greece)

Metered Mail (early GB meter mark)

Military Franchise Stamps

METAL CURRENCY STAMPS. Stamps so designated could only be purchased in hard currency - gold or silver - as opposed to stamps for internal mail, tariffed in depreciating paper currency. Peruvian stamps were overprinted "Plata" (Spanish for silver) in 1880, for this reason. Similarly Greek stamps inscribed or overprinted AM (*Axia Metallike* = metal value) were issued for use on foreign parcels which had to be prepaid at the "gold" exchange rate.

METALLIC INK. Copper-bronze and bronze-gold inks were first used by Switzerland (1867–82) while gold ink was used by Holland (1867–71). The first stamps printed entirely in metallic ink were the Greek drachmae values of 1901, bronze, silver and gold inks being used in ascending order of value. Otherwise metallic ink was used very sparingly - by El Salvador and New South Wales (1897), the Persian coronation set (1915) and South Africa's Rand 2'd (1938) and Royal Silver Wedding stamps (1948). Since the 1960s, however, it has been widely used in multicolour offset and photogravure printing. *See also* Foil stamps. ∎

METERED MAIL. Mail on which the postage is indicated by marks applied by postage meter. This system was pioneered by New Zealand and the United States at the beginning of this century, but expanded considerably from 1922 when interna-

tional acceptance of metered mail was sanctioned by the Universal Postal Union. Meter marks are usually applied in red ink, and include an indication of the country of issue, value and licence number, a dater die and often a slogan advertising the user.

MILITARY EXPEDITIONS. *See* Expedition Stamps.

MILITARY FRANCHISE STAMPS. Stamps permitting forces on active service to send letters, cards and parcels free of postage. Stamps of this type were first issued by Brazil during the war of 1865–70 against Paraguay. Free postage was granted to Spanish troops in Morocco (1893–4) and labels inscribed "Melilla" were produced privately and distributed to the troops. Major Kenyon produced a set of three labels inscribed "Army Frank" for the use of troops during the Spanish-American War (1898). Other semi-official stamps of this type include the prolific issues of the Swiss Army. British forces in the Canal Zone used NAAFI seals and concessionary stamps to send mail home at reduced rates (1932–6), prior to the issue of the Army Post stamps by Egypt. French stamps overprinted or inscribed FM (*Franchise Militaire*) and Danish stamps overprinted SF (*Soldater Frimaerke*), German stamps inscribed "Luftfeldpost" (air field post) and American $1 stamps of 1968 inscribed "Airlift" are among other issues in this category.

Military Telegraphs (GB 2d. and ½d. overprinted)

Millésime (France and Colonies, numerals signifying year of printing)

MILITARY POSTS. Postal services organised on behalf of troops on active service date from the Napoleonic Wars, special postmarks being used by both Britain and France in this connexion. Distinctive postmarks were also used during the Crimean War (1853–6) and the Egyptian campaign (1882), the Royal Engineers Postal Corps being formed at that time. Military postmarks associated with the Franco-German War (1870–1) include some of the earliest types of postcard, just as some of the earliest **aerogrammes** were produced for servicemen in the Second World War. Stamps for the use of troops on active service, as opposed to **Military Franchise** stamps, were first issued in 1879 for the use of Austro-Hungarian forces in the Turkish provinces of Bosnia and Herzegovina, the service being later extended to the civilian population. These stamps were inscribed K.U.K. MILITARPOST (Royal and Imperial Military Post) and continued until the end of the First World War. Austria also issued stamps inscribed FELDPOST (field post) for use in territories occupied during the First World War. Details of other military posts will be found listed under Expedition stamps. *See also* Airgraph, Campaign cover, Censor marks and labels, Honour envelopes, Miliary Franchise stamps, Patriotic covers, Propaganda leaflets, Siege postmarks and stamps, V mail and War stamps.

MILITARY TELEGRAPHS. Stamps from the unappropriated dies overprinted MILITARY TELEGRAPHS were provided by Somerset House for the use of British troops in Egypt (1884–7), Bechuanaland (1885) and the Sudan (1885). Stamps of the Cape of Good Hope (1885) and the Sudan (1896) were also overprinted for this purpose. During both World Wars and in subsequent years special datestamps inscribed "Army Signals" were used on military telegrams.

MILLÉSIME. Numerals recording the year of printing certain stamps of France and Colonies, the final digit of the year being printed in the interpane gutters.

MINIATURE SHEET. A small sheet containing a single stamp, pair, block or set of stamps, with wide, inscribed and/

Miniature Sheet (East Germany, 1983)

1

2

3

4

5

6

7

1 Abnormal – GB 1865 9d. from plate 5.
2 Anaglyph – one of only two stamps printed
in this way. **3** Aniline colour – Brazilian
stamps. **4** Blue Safety Paper – GB 1d. fiscal
stamp, 1853. **5** Blued Paper – GB 1841 1d. red.
6 Boule de Moulins – shown on French stamp,
1979. **7** Burelage – Queensland and Albania
issues.

1 Cardboard – German and GB imprinted stamps from postcards. **2** Cartridge paper – Russia, 1921. **3** Chalk-surfaced Paper – Dominica, 1923. **4** Cleaned – Cape cancel removed; Tasmania pen marks removed. **5** Collotype – Queensland, New South Wales and St Vincent.

1

2

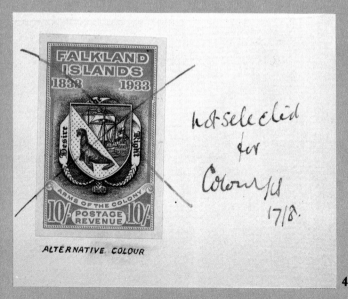

ALTERNATIVE COLOUR

4

3

1 Colour Changeling – Brazil 100r. of 1882 – normal olive-green and changeling orange-brown; GB ½d. of 1900 – normal green and changeling blue. **2** Colour Fake – US stamp in normal purple and with colour changed by chemical action. **3** Colour Proof – Honduras; France 'Peace and Commerce' and 'Sower' types. **4** Colour Trial – Falkland Is. 1933 10s. stamp 'not selected for colour'.

1

2

3

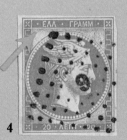

4

1 Coloured Papers – Surface-coloured (Russia, French Guinea); paper coloured throughout (St Vincent, British Honduras). **2** Coloured Postmark – 1970 London International Stamp Exhibition, Philympia. **3** Coupon Paper – Lithuania, 1919. **4** Découpage – Greece, 1872 – découpage too low and too far to right.

1 'Silk threads' in GB Victorian embossed stamp. **2** Die Proofs – GB George V 1d. stamp; Mauritius (Admiral de Labour-donnais). **3** Double Print – Sweden 20 ore very pale orange and double print in pale orange and vermilion, 1875–6. **4** Dry Print – GB George VI 2d. **5** Enamelled Paper – Portugal, 1894. **6** Engraver's Progress Proof – Western Australia partially completed proof of the 1d. 'Swan'.

1 Essay – Denmark; Andorra; GB 1839 'Treasury' essay. **2** Fluorescence – Security devices on Norfolk Island and Hong Kong stamps. **3** Foil Stamp – Russia, silver foil paper, 1965.

1

2

3

4

1 Forgery – Gold Coast 4d. and 6d. of the 1880s. **2** Fugitive Inks – GB and Perak stamps damaged by attempts to tamper with them. **3** Glazed Paper – Russia. **4** Goldbeater's Skin – German 1886 parcel stamp.

1 Grand Consommation – French stamps printed on pale grey granite emergency paper. **2** Granite Paper – Swiss booklet pane, 1924.

1 Grille – security device on US and Peruvian stamps.   **2** Gum – ribbed, white, gum arabic, polyvinyl alcohol, dextrine.

1 Gum Device – Czechoslovakia 1923 'CSP' emblem on gum.   **2** Hand-made Paper – Travancore (Indian Feudatory State); GB 2d. blue; Austria.   **3** Hand-painted – red 'printing' added, Germany 1900 5m.   **4** Helecon – Australia's 1963 'Rabbit Bandicoot' stamp, the first printed on Helecon paper.   **5** Imprimatur – GB 1880 1d. Venetian red.   **6** India-Paper – France 'Mouchon' proof.

1

2

3

4

1 Ink – inking faults on stamps of Ceylon, South Africa and Switzerland. **2** Ivory Head – GB 1d. red and 2d. blue. **3** Japanese Paper – Japan 1872 'Cherry Blossom' issue. **4** Letterpress – stamps of Russia, Portugal, Australia and Netherlands.

LINE BLOCK/LITHOGRAPHY

1

2

3

1

2

3

4

5

(*Opposite plate*) **1** Line Block – New Zealand. **2** Line Engraving – recess-printed stamps of Bermuda, GB, British Guiana, Falkland Islands, France. **3** Lithography – stamps of GB, Newfoundland, Surinam.

1 Luminescence – US stamp on luminescent 'Hi Brite' paper. **2** Manilla Paper – Swedish military post envelope. **3** Matched Pair – GB 1d. black and 1d. red, plate VIII showing the 'Q' flaw, corner letters 'EC'. **4** Metallic Ink – gold and silver inks on South African stamps, 1938, 1948. **5** Mirror Print – complete set-off on Italian stamp (with normal) and part set-off on Turks and Caicos Islands stamp.

1 Mixed Printing – Chile (engraved and litho), USA (recess and litho), Chile (litho and typo), Uruguay (half-tone and line-block). **2** Moiré – security device on British Honduras stamp. **3** Mounted mint – lightly and heavily mounted unused stamps.

1

2

3

4

1 Native Paper – Portugal (postage due), Bhor, Kashmir (Indian Feudatory State), Tibet. **2** Palimpsest – Mexico, 1874 25c. **3** Paper Error – Hungary 1913 60f. olive-green on white; 60f. olive-green on rose. **4** Pelure – semi-transparent paper used for stamps of Serbia and Russia.

1 Phosphor – Canadian 'Tagged' stamps; GB 1975 8½p. Christmas stamp with phosphor ink background; 1p. Machin stamp on phosphorised paper.   **2** Photography – Mafeking 1900 1d. local post stamp.   **3** Photogravure – Single colour and multicoloured photogravure stamps.

GSM Competition (March)
Stanley Gibbons Magazine Ltd.,
5 Parkside,
Christchurch Road,
RINGWOOD,
Hants.
BH24 3SH

1

2

3

1 Phosphor Dots – Blue postcode dots, introduced in 1978.   **2** Plate Proof – Argentina (line-engraved); Rumania 3b. – pair electro-typed in colour.   **3** Porous Paper – Nicaragua, 1873.

1 Postal Union Colours – GB Edward VII, USA 'Presidents', France 'Sower'.
2 Premières Gravures – USA 3c. President stamp original and amended printings. Latter with additional 'ball' in each corner.   **3** Printer's Waste – Montenegro 1896, misprinted and 'blue-pencilled'; Spain 2c. of 1874 – lemon-yellow colour misapplied and inverted on 5c. mauve.

1 Rainbow Trials – GB 1d. red of May 1841.   **2** Re-engraving – original and re-engraved stamps of Canada.   **3** Repp paper – stamp of Austrian Lombardy and Venetia printed on 'corrugated paper'. **4** Rice Paper – Salvador, 1889.   **5** Ruled Paper – Latvia (1919) and Mexico (1887).   **6** Safety Paper – Prussian stamp with 'burelage revealed'.   **7** Set-Off – Rhodesia; Colombia.

1

2

3

4

1 Shade – USA 2c.; Sweden 5 ore. **2** Silk-thread Paper – GB Victorian postal stationery envelope. **3** Slurred Print – USA; Mexico; Newfoundland. **4** Stamped Paper – GB embossed revenue stamp 'Bill or note'.

1

2

3

1 Sulphuretted – 'oxidised' stamps of Peru, GB, Canada, China and Newfoundland.   **2** Textiles as Printing Materials – Bhutan stamp printed on silk rayon, 1969.   **3** Thermography – Sierra Leone surcharges, 1965.

1

1 Thermoplastics – Bhutan stamps with 3-D effect.   **2** Tinted Paper – Belgian stamp printed on lightly toned paper.

2

2

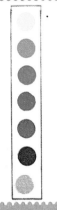

1

1 Traffic Lights – modern GB commemoratives. **2** Undenominated stamps of USA (1985) and Canada (1981). **3** Value Converted – Mexico, 1916.

3

1 Value Erased – Corrientes 1867 (2c.) black on lemon-yellow.
2 Value Inserted – Barbacoas (Colombia) type-set stamp (1901–3) with value and dated added in manuscript. **3** Varnish Lines – Austrian stamp of 1901–7 with diagonal varnish lines. **4** Worn Plate – Argentina (normal and pair from worn plate); Venezuela; GB 1d. red. **5** Xylography – Victoria 'woodblock' stamps, 1854–9.

or decorative margins, issued as a commemorative souvenir for collectors. The first miniature sheets were issued by Luxembourg (1923) and Belgium (1924). Since then they have spread to most countries, although it was not until 1978 that Britain issued its first sheet. Sometimes the stamps in such sheets differ in colour, value or perforation from those issued in more conventional sheet form. *See also* Souvenir sheet.

MINT. A stamp in its original state of issue, unused and with full gum (if so issued).

MIRROR PRINT. A proof from a die made in relief for stereotypes and therefore a negative image of the finished stamp. The term also applies to impressions set-off on the backs of sheets of stamps, caused by wet ink adhering from another sheet during printing. ■

MIXED FOUNTS. The employment of several different founts of type in **overprints** or **typeset stamps**.

Mixed Founts (Perak; Sonora, Mexico; Selangor)

MIXED FRANKING. More properly "mixed postage", the term used by collectors to denote covers or postcards bearing the stamps of two or more different countries or regimes. The term is also used (*Mischfrankatur*) in Germany to denote postal items bearing stamps from two different issues, usually in the period before the earlier issue is demonetised, but has been rendered obsolescent by the introduction of the later series.

MIXED PERFORATION. Defectively perforated stamps which have been patched on their backs and re-perforated,

usually resulting in compound perforations. Notable examples are the New Zealand issues of 1901.

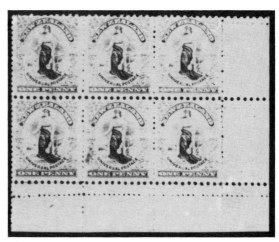

Mixed Perforation (New Zealand)

MIXED PRINTING. The use of more than one printing process in the production of stamps. Thus one may find combinations of intaglio and photogravure, lithography and letterpress, or intaglio and letterpress in some British commemoratives since 1973. Austria, Czechoslovakia, Belgium, the United States and Russia, among others, have used intaglio combined with photogravure in recent years. Chile has had stamps with engraved heads and lithographed frames, while Uruguay has used half-tone vignettes and line-block frames. Intaglio has been combined with lithography (Vietnam) or letterpress (Poland). ■

Mobile Post Office (GB postmark for Mobile PO No. 1)

MOBILE POST OFFICE. A vehicle fully equipped as a post office, used at fairs, exhibitions, sporting events and other venues where postal facilities are temporarily required. Offices of this type have been used in Britain for many years, using handstamps inscribed M.P.O. or "Mobile Post Office" followed by a number. Many offices of this type were prepared during the Second World War, to be used in emergencies if permanent offices were destroyed by enemy action. Similar temporary offices are used at special events in other countries - not to be confused with **highway post offices** which provide a regular service on cross-country routes in rural areas of the USA, Switzerland, etc.

MOIRÉ. A pattern of close-set wavy lines simulating watered silk, printed on postage stamps as a security feature. Examples may be seen on the backs of Mexican stamps (1872) and overprinted on stamps of British Honduras during the First World War. *See also* Burelage.   ∎

MONEY, STAMPS AS. *See* Currency stamps, Encased Postage stamps, Postage Currency and Fractional Currency.

MOUNTED MINT. Unused stamps showing traces of stamp mounts or hinges on their backs.   ∎

MOURNING STAMPS. Stamps issued on occasions of national bereavement, either special issues printed in black, or existing stamps having an added black border. The Courier Stadtbrief Beforderung, a German local post, issued black stamps in mourning for the Emperor Wilhelm I and his son Friedrich III, both of whom died in 1888. The first mourning stamps by a government postal administration were the US 2c stamps of 1923 honouring Warren Harding. Russia issued mourning stamps for Lenin in 1924–8.

Mourning Stamps (Belgium, Lithuania, Russia)

MOVABLE BOX. A special posting box on the deck of cross-Channel steamers, plying between England, the Channel Islands and France. Such boxes were removed at the port of destination and their contents processed by the nearest post office, which used a special postmark inscribed M.B. (Movable Box) or B.M. (*Boite Mobile*). This practice began in the 1840s and was regularised by the Anglo-French Postal Convention of 1856. The service was discontinued on the outbreak of the Second World War.

Movable Box—postmark and cover

MULREADY. Postal stationery, in the form of wrappers and letter sheets, issued by Britain in 1840, and deriving its name from William Mulready who designed the ornate allegorical motif which decorated the address portion. Mulready's pompous design, showing Britannia sending forth her messengers to all parts of the globe, was ridiculed and lampooned, and became the subject of numerous caricatures sold by stationers. The Mulready stationery was replaced by embossed covers and letter sheets in 1841, but inadvertently triggered off the mid-Victorian fashion for pictorial stationery.

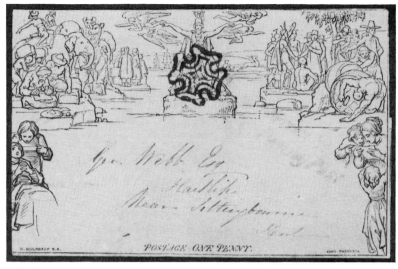

Mulready envelope

Multilingual Stamps (Switzerland—German, French, Italian)

MULTILINGUAL POSTMARKS AND STAMPS. Postmarks and stamps inscribed in two or more languages. In Britain some special event handstamps and slogans have been used in Welsh, Scots Gaelic, Latin and even Anglo-Saxon, in addition to the normal English, and postage stamps have occasionally included Welsh inscriptions. Both Welsh and Gaelic have been used on aerogrammes issued in Wales and Scotland, and Welsh is employed on some postal labels, such as **Recorded Delivery**. In other countries, multilingual stamps and postmarks are much more common, often reflecting the linguistic and ethnic mixture of their peoples. Stamps issued simultaneously in two languages were pioneered by Switerland in 1850, and in three languages by the same country in 1939–42. Stamps with bilingual inscriptions have long been issued by Belgium, Canada and South Africa, as well as many Slavonic and Oriental countries which include French in accordance with UPU regulations, as well as their own script. *See also* Bilingual Pairs, Trilingual Strips.

Multiple Watermark (Persia—arms; Commonwealth Multiple Crown CA and Multiple Script CA)

MULTIPLE WATERMARK. A watermark device repeated all over the sheet, so that each stamp may show several devices in whole or part.

MULTIPOSITIVE. Image produced by the "step and repeat" process from a master negative, and then transferred to the printing cylinder for **photogravure**.

MUTILATION. Cancellation of stamps by tearing, scratching or cutting off a portion of the design. This method was used in the case of the Lady McLeod local service of Trinidad (1847) and the early stamps of Afghanistan.

Mutilation (early Afghan issues had section torn off and pen cancel)

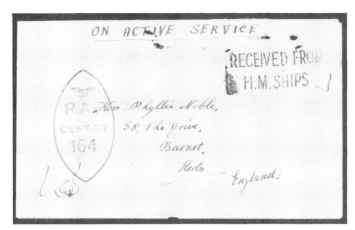

Naval Mail (GB—Received From HM Ships, also censor mark)

NAPHTHADAG. Trade name composed of Naphtha and DAG, an acronym from Deflocculated Acheson's Graphite, to denote the black substance used for the **graphite lines** printed on the back of some British stamps issued in 1957 in connexion with automatic sorting experiments at Southampton.

NATIVE PAPER. A general term indicating locally-made paper used for the stamps of some of the Indian states and the countries of the Far East. Usually tough and fibrous, varying greatly in texture and thickness. ∎

NAVAL MAIL. Correspondence conveyed by or landed from naval vessels, usually though not invariably in wartime. Special postmarks, such as **dumb cancellations** or denoting exemption from postal charges, **censor marks** or distinctive shipboard handstamps (e.g. those used by the US Navy, the German Marineschiffspost and the French Navy), may characterise such items. Stamps have also been produced aboard warships, e.g. Rouad (1915), Mount Athos (1916) and Bouvet Island (1934), or in connexion with naval expeditions, e.g. Castellorizo (1915) and Long Island (1916). *See also* Submarine Mail.

NEWSPAPER STAMPS. Stamps issued specifically to denote the prepayment of postage on newspapers and periodicals. This category, incidentally, includes some of the largest (USA) and smallest (Australian states) stamps ever issued. Distinctive stamps inscribed "Newspaper Postage", or its equivalent in other languages, have been issued by Austria, Germany, Czechoslovakia and New Zealand. Britain's small-sized halfpenny stamp of 1870 was introduced primarily for this purpose, although not thus inscribed.

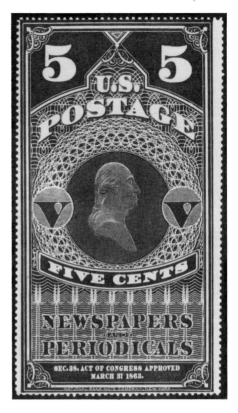

Newspaper Stamps (the US stamp is one of the largest ever issued)

NEWSPAPER TAX STAMPS. Impressed or adhesive stamps denoting the payment of taxes on newspapers and other periodicals, used by many European countries as a means of raising revenue and curbing the freedom of the press. Such stamps, impressed on the upper corner of the front page, were used in the UK from 1712 till 1870 when this "tax on knowledge" was finally abolished. As the payment of this tax entitled the papers to be transmitted and re-transmitted through the post without further charge, it has been argued that they also served as a form of postage stamp. From 1855 to 1870 they were only payable in respect of papers sent by post and therefore should be regarded in that period purely as postage stamps. Several papers (*The Times*, the *Illustrated London News* and *Stamford Mercury*) elected to use precancelled black impressed stamps after 1855 as an alternative to adhesive stamps, on copies sent by post. Austria issued adhesive tax stamps, inscribed ZEITUNGS STEMPEL, to distinguish them from newspaper postage stamps (inscribed ZEITUNGS POST STEMPEL). French tax stamps were affixed to the page prior to printing, so that newsprint served to cancel the stamps and prevent re-use.

Newspaper Tax Stamps (GB, in use 1712–1870)

NIGHTRIDER. A special overnight parcel delivery service of the British Post Office, confined to the London Postal Region and distinguished by labels thus inscribed.

Nightrider label—London overnight parcel service

NOT FOR USE. Overprint applied to 1d stamps of Natal about 1910. **Booklets** containing thirty 1d stamps were sold for 2s6d, but the customer was charged 1d for the booklet, and thus one of the stamps was overprinted in this manner to render it invalid for postal use.

NPM CARDS. Picture postcards published by the National Postal Museum, London, illustrating historic postage stamps, postmarks and subjects of postal historical interest. *See also* PHQ Cards.

NUMBERED STAMPS. Stamps bearing serial numbers as part of their design, or printed on the back. Estonia's liberation stamps of 1927 were numbered in rotation throughout the sheet, while Uruguay's 1882 issue likewise showed different numerals below the central motif. Many stamps of Spain and colonies from 1875 were serially numbered on the back, stamps having an all-zero serial being **specimens**. France began serially numbering every tenth stamp in **coils** in 1966, a practice since adopted by some other countries. Greek stamps (1861–80) were numbered on the back to indicate the denomination and facilitate handling by postal staff.

NUMERAL CANCELLATIONS. Obliterations which incorporate numbers as a means of identifying the office of posting. In the U.K. they superseded the **Maltese Cross** in 1844, separate sets of numbers being allocated to the London Chief Office, the London District Post, the provincial offices of England and Wales, and both Ireland and Scotland. These numbers were later used in **duplex** and **double stamps** and (in Scotland and a few English offices) also in combined stamps (1883–1956). Numbered obliterators were also used in many European countries, as well as Canada, the Australian states, India and some British colonies.

NPM Cards (GB National Postal Museum card, issued 1983)

Not For Use (Natal, c. 1910)

Numbered Stamps (Uruguay, Spain)

Numeral Cancellations (GB Penny Reds with numeral cancels of London and the provinces; Netherlands)

OBLIGATORY STAMPS. *See* Compulsory Postage.

OBLIQUE ROULETTE. Otherwise known as *percé en lignes obliques*, it is a rare type of separation in which the cuts are aslant and parallel. Such stamps are not easily separated, and the edges of detached stamps are usually rough and irregular. This type of separation was used by Van Diemen's Land (Tasmania).

Oblique Roulette (Van Diemen's Land = Tasmania)

OBLITERATION. Synonym for **cancellation** but usually employed to denote the thorough defacement of a stamp by means of a **"killer"** to prevent re-use. In Post Office parlance, the obliterator, or obliterating element, of a postmark is that part designed purely to prevent re-use, as opposed to the dater die which gives the name of the office and the date of posting.

Obliteration (early US 'killer' postmarks)

OBSOLETE. No longer available over the post office counter, but still valid for postage. American stamps, for example, from 1861 onwards may be obsolete, but are still postally valid. Similarly, British stamps are normally retained at philatelic counters for twelve months after they have been withdrawn from general sale; but all stamps issued since 1971 remain postally valid.

Obsolete stamps—no longer on sale at post offices but still valid for postage

OCCUPATION STAMPS. Stamps overprinted or specially printed for use in a territory occupied by military forces other than its own, during or after a period of war. Stamps of this type were first issued in 1864 by the German Federal Commissioners in the duchy of Holstein, following the invasion by Austro-Prussian forces. Subsequently stamps were issued during the occupation of Alsace-Lorraine (1870), Peru (1878–83), Thessaly (1895), Cuba, Porto Rico and the Philippines (1898–1900), Crete (1898), the Orange Free State and the Transvaal (1900–2), the Dodecanese Islands (1912), Macedonia and Thrace (1913), as well as numerous territories in both world wars and other campaigns of more recent years. *See also* Expedition stamps, Military and Naval mail.

Occupation Stamps (First and Second World Wars)

OFF CENTRE. A term used to denote inaccurate perforation, resulting in unequal margins around a stamp. In extreme cases the perforation actually cuts into the stamp design.

Official Mail (registered cover from Rumanian PO, complete with string and metal seal)

OFFICIAL MAIL. Correspondence of government departments, members of parliament, officers of state and royal households, subject to special handling and often exempted from postal charges. Such mail may enjoy a **franking privilege** by signature endorsement or by means of a **certifying stamp**; or it may be denoted by means of **Official Paid stationery**, **postmarks** or **stamps** the improper use of which, however, may entail a **penalty**. *See also* Departmental stamps and Interpostal seals.

OFFICIAL PAID STATIONERY. Postal stationery provided for the use of government departments, or as a means whereby the public can reply to government offices. In the latter category, stationery bore impressed or embossed stamps in Britain until 1904, but from 1903 till 1983 printed devices inscribed OFFICIAL PAID, with or without a crown, were used. Similar stationery is, or has been, used in many other countries, sometimes with an impressed stamp or logo, and a superscription signifying that it is on state or government service.

Official Paid Stationery

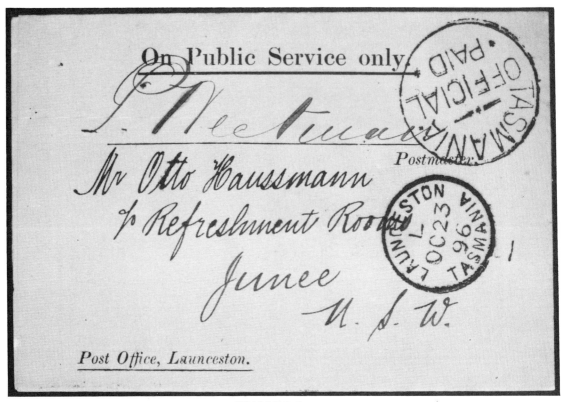

Official Paid Stationery

OFFICIAL STAMPS. Postage stamps provided for use on official correspondence. Where they are inscribed or overprinted for the use of specific departments they are known as **Departmental stamps**. The famous VR Penny Black of 1840, prepared for use but never issued, was intended for this purpose. Official stamps may be recognised by their inscription or overprint, e.g. "Service", "Dienstmarke", "Tjaneste", "Offentlig Sak" or variants of "Official" itself.·

Official Stamps (India, Spain, Trinidad, Costa Rica, Dominican Republic, Uruguay)

OFFSET LITHOGRAPHY. A modern variant of lithography in which the image is photographed on to a flexible zinc or aluminium plate which, after processing, is curved around a cylinder for use in a rotary press. The revolving, inked cylinder is brought in close contact with a blanket roller which receives a reversed impression of the original plate of stamp images. These are transferred in turn by offset contact with the paper which is fed by the impression cylinder. A variant of this, patented by De La Rue, is known as **Delacryl**.

OMNIBUS ISSUE. An issue of stamps made by a number of countries simultaneously to commemorate the same person or event, and formerly using uniform designs. The first omnibus issue was made in 1898 by Portugal and her overseas colonies for the quatercentenary of Vasco da Gama's discovery of the sea route to India. Subsequently France (1931) and the British crown colonies (1935) produced omnibus issues. The latter continued to use uniform designs till 1967, but since then greater variety has been imparted by using distinctive motifs, although they tend to have uniform frames.

ORIGINAL GUM. Sometimes abbreviated to O.G., it denotes a stamp which still possesses all or some of the **gum** which was present at the time of issue.

OVERALL MULTIPLE WATERMARK. A network pattern watermark covering all stamps in a sheet.

OVERLAND MAIL. A postal service operated between India and Britain by Thomas Waghorn who relied on an overland route across Egypt from Suez to Alexandria to accelerate the mail (1829–50). The term was also used for the trans-continental mail by stage coach across the United States in the 1860s. Special labels thus inscribed were used on the mail conveyed across the desert between Baghdad and Haifa by Nairn Transport Ltd in 1923.

Omnibus Issues (1953 Coronation, 1966 Churchill commemoration)

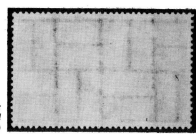

Overall Multiple Watermark (Thailand 'rectangles')

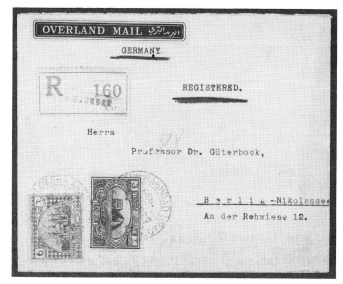

Overland Mail (Iraq–Germany cover with Overland Mail label)

OVERPRINT. An inscription or device added to the face of a stamp subsequent to the original printing. Such an inscription may be added to alter the purpose, or place of validity, or to commemorate an event or anniversary. Where the additional inscription changes the face value of the stamp, this is termed a **surcharge**. *See also* Continuous and Security overprint.

Overprint (War Tax, Commemorative, Political change)

OXIDISED. *See* Sulphuretted.

PACKET LETTER. An item of mail brought ashore from a packet, that is a ship either maintained by the government or carrying mail under Post Office contract, as distinct from a **Ship letter**. Packet Letter postmarks were used at many British ports in the 19th and early 20th centuries, notably the series employed at Falmouth which indicated the port of despatch as well.

Packet Letter—Devonport, Plymouth, Liverpool postmarks

PAID POSTMARK. A postmark, usually though not always applied in red ink, indicating the prepayment of postage in cash, as opposed to adhesive or impressed postage stamps. As such, they may be regarded as **handstruck postage stamps**. They date from 1680 when William **Dockwra** introduced his London Penny Post, and reached their peak in 1840, with the advent of Uniform Penny Postage which encouraged the prepayment of postage. They continue in use to this day, but since 1852 have been confined in Britain to **bulk posting**. Both handstruck and machine marks are used. Other forms of paid postmark include those used on **metered** and **permit** mail. *See also* Mailomat, Official Mail and Postage Paid Impressions.

Paid Postmark (Manchester, 1971)

PAIR. Two unsevered stamps, joined horizontally or vertically.

Pair (GB, France)

Pane of GB Victorian stamps

PALIMPSEST. A manuscript in which original writing has been erased to make way for new. The term is used philatelically to describe the erasure of part of a design, usually a value or inscription, but where vestiges of the original remain and can be seen below or alongside the revised inscription. *See also* Erased. ■

PANE. The sub-section or part of a sheet of stamps, usually separated by **gutter** margins and often cut up prior to issue to the public. It also describes the leaf comprising two or more stamps issued in booklets.

Paper-Maker's Watermark (Harrisons & Sons Ltd—Maldive Is.)

Paquebot—Port Said cancel on British stamp

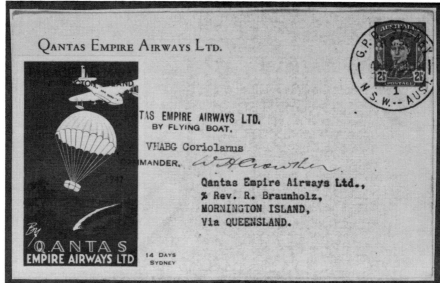

Parachute Mail (Mornington Island, Australia, 1942)

PAPER. Material of closely compacted vegetable (wood or cloth) fibres, first used as a writing material by the Chinese in the 2nd century BC, by the Arabs in 751 AD, and in western Europe about 1100. The earliest letter written on paper preserved in the Public Record Office, London is dated 1216. Many different kinds of paper have been used in the manufacture of postage stamps and postal stationery and may be found under Banknote, Batonne, Blued, Blue Safety, Cardboard, Chalk-surfaced, Chalky, Cigarette, Coloured, Coupon, Dickinson, Double, Glazed, Grand Consommation, Granite, Handmade, India, Japanese, Laid, Manilla, Native, Pelure, Phosphor, Porous, Quadrille, Repaired, Repp, Resinised, Ribbed, Rice, Ruled, Safety, Sensitised, Silk, Varnished, Winchester and Wove paper.

PAPER ERROR. Stamps printed on paper of the wrong colour (intended for another denomination), or printed on paper specially watermarked for another value or issue. ■

PAPER-MAKER'S WATERMARK. A normal watermark incorporating the paper-maker's name, brand name or trademark.

PAQUEBOT. French word derived from "Packet Boat" and adopted by the Universal Postal Union in 1894 to denote mail posted on board ship and subsequently taken ashore for onward transmission. Distinctive Paquebot postmarks are used at many ports to cancel mail which may often bear the postage stamps of other countries. *See also* Loose Letter, Packet Letter and Ship Letter.

PARACHUTE MAIL. A form of airmail in which mail is delivered by free-fall parachute from an aeroplane. Used extensively to supply remote combat units during the Second World War, it has since been used in peacetime to drop mail to islands such as Mornington Island, Rotuma and St Kilda, special **cachets** being used on these occasions.

PARAPH. A mark or flourish, used in embellishment, or, in the form of initials, as a signature. Found overprinted on Cuban stamps used in Puerto Rico (1873–6) and on Mexican stamps,

PARCEL LABEL. Adhesive label of a distinctive type, issued to every post office in the United Kingdom in August 1883 and employed on parcels until 1918. Since then anonymous labels have been used, but only at the smaller post offices that do not have a **parcel postmark**. As each office had its own distinctive labels, and several types were produced in the 35 years of usage, it follows that this is a vast field of research for the postal historian. Many other types of label have been used

in connexion with parcel services throughout the world. *See also* Nightrider, Trakback.

PARCEL POSTMARK. A postal marking used in connexion with the parcel post. In the UK undated cork cancels were used to cancel adhesive stamps on parcel labels (1883–5), but were followed by rubber stamps showing the name but without a date. Later on various rollers or **rotary cancellations** were used. Facsimile label rubber datestamps have also been used at the larger post offices and gradually ousted parcel labels. Special postmarks applied in ink, and usually oval in shape, are used on parcels posted in bulk and prepaid in cash. In recent years **Postage Paid Impressions** have been used for the same purpose. Distinctive postmarks for parcel service are also used in many other countries.

Parcel Label (Marchmont St Post Office, 1899)

Paraph (Puerto Rico, Mexico)

Parcel Postmark (GB)

PARCEL STAMPS. Stamps designated or inscribed for use on parcels were produced by freight companies long before adhesive stamps were used by government postal services, and are believed to date from 1821, if not earlier. The railway companies also produced their own parcel stamps from the 1840s onwards, and both carriers and bus companies continue to issue them to this day. The first parcel stamps under government auspices were issued by the Belgian State Railways (1879). Britain's first stamp specifically for parcels was the 9d definitive of 1883, and stamps overprinted at the same time for use on Government Parcels. Italy introduced parcel stamps in 1884 and since 1914 these have been **bi-partite**. The USA adopted parcel stamps of pictorial designs in 1912, and also issued parcel postage due labels. The Vatican has issued stamps for **express parcels**.

Uruguay—farm produce parcel stamp

Parcel Stamps—Belgian railway issues

PARLIAMENTARY STAMPS AND STATIONERY. When the **franking privilege** was withdrawn in 1840, special covers were provided for the Houses of Parliament, pending the introduction of the **certifying stamp** system. Parliamentary envelopes were revived in 1983 when **Official Paid stationery** was abolished. Distinctive stationery, exempt from normal postal charges, has also been issued by many other countries. Adhesive stamps for parliamentary use were issued by Spain (1895–8) and inscribed "Congreso de los Disputados" (Congress of Deputies). Since 1950 stamps have been provided for the use of delegates and permanent officials of the Council of Europe, Strasbourg, on official correspondence.

After 1960, however, the use of these stamps was extended to all mail posted at the Council building.

Parliamentary stamp (Spain)

PART IMPRESSION. A stamp which has received only a partial impression from the printing plate or cylinder, due to a production fault. This may arise from underinking or from paper being folded over, or from extraneous matter adhering to the paper or plate during printing and subsequently falling away.

Part Impression (Brazil, part of red colour missing)

PART PERFORATION. An irregularity caused by missing, blunt or defective pins in the perforator, or from the perforator inadvertently missing a row or rows. This gives rise to the variety known as **Imperforate Between**.

Part Perforation (Greece, Mexico)

PATRIOTIC COVER. Envelope decorated, with pictures and slogans of a patriotic nature. They first appeared during the American Civil War (1861–5) and were used to a lesser extent during the Franco-German War (1870–1). They became very fashionable during the Boer War, being especially popular in Canada and New Zealand. They were less extensive during the First World War but made a come-back during the Second World War, particularly in the USA and Canada.

PELURE. French word denoting a very thin, hard and tough paper, usually semi-transparent, employed for the stamps of New Zealand, Serbia and Russia among others. ■

Patriotic Covers

PEN CANCELLED. *See* Manuscript Cancellation.

PENALTY STAMPS AND STATIONERY. Stationery intended for use on official correspondence is thus designated in the United States on account of the warning printed on such envelopes and cards, that improper or unauthorised use may incur a penalty up to $300. When adhesive stamps were introduced in 1983 these likewise bore an inscription "Penalty for private use $300" - a sum which, incidentally, has remained at that level for over a century.

Penmarked (GB, New Zealand)

Penalty Stamp (USA—$300 fine for unathorised use)

PENMARKED. A stamp defaced by pen marks for other than postal purposes, e.g. fiscal use, documents, bills, receipts, etc.

PENNY POST. A postal service delivering letters and packets within a certain limited area for a penny each. This was pioneered in London by William **Dockwra** in 1680, his service being nationalised two years later. Penny posts spread to Dublin (1773) and Edinburgh (1774) and other provincial towns and cities at the beginning of the 19th century. By the 1830s local penny posts existed in many parts of the British Isles. Uniform Penny Post, with a basic rate of 1d per half ounce irrespective of distance carried, was introduced in the UK in January 1840 and continued till 1918 when it became a casualty of wartime costs. Distinctive postmarks associated with the local penny posts are much sought after by postal historians.

PERCÉ. French word meaning "pierced". *See* Roulette.

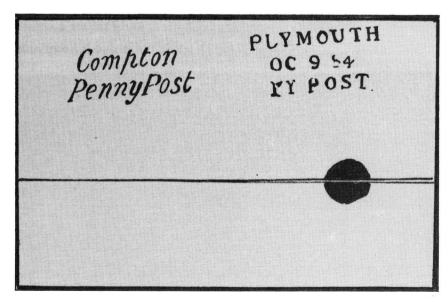

Penny Post Marking

Perfins (PAC on the GB 5d stamp = Pearl Assurance Company)

Permit Mail (Australia, New Zealand, USA)

PERFINS. Stamps perforated with the initials or emblems of firms, sometimes known to collectors as "Spifs" or "branded" stamps. These are now receiving the serious attention of collectors, particularly local historians who attempt to identify the users. These stamps were perforated as a security measure, to prevent pilferage by office staff. In the UK, although largely superseded by metered mail, they are still occasionally encountered, usually on mail sent by local authorities. Stamps perforated in this way for the use of government departments should be classed as **Official stamps**.

PERFORATION. A series of holes punched between stamps in the sheet to facilitate separation, the tiny discs of paper being removed, as opposed to **rouletting** in which the paper is merely cut or pierced. *See also* Automatic Machine, Blind, Clean-cut, Comb, Compound, Error, Fake, Harrow, Imitation, Intermediate, Interrupted, Irregular, Line, Mixed, Private, Rotary, Rough, Sewing-machine and Unusual perforations.

PERMIT MAIL. Third and fourth class mail (bulk postings of printed matter) which the USPO has permitted private firms to despatch since April 1904 with various types of handstruck or printed impressions denoting prepayment of postage. These impressions show the town name, the permit number, the class of mail, the value and often the relevant section of the Postal Laws and Regulations governing the different classes of mail. The earliest Pitney-Bowes machines were, in fact, developed for use in permit mailing, and extended to **metered mail** in 1920. Permit mail has continued to be an important aspect of bulk posting, and subsequently spread to Canada and New Zealand. A somewhat similar system is now used in many other countries. *See also* Postage Paid Impressions.

PERSONAL DELIVERY. Czechoslovakia (1937 and 1946) and Bohemia and Moravia (1939) issued triangular stamps of two types. Those in red, inscribed D, represented a fee payable by an addressee who required all his mail to be delivered to him personally. These stamps were affixed by the delivery office to all such items. Those in blue, inscribed V, were used to ensure personal delivery to the addressee, and affixed by the sender.

Personal Delivery (Czechoslovakia, 1937)

PHANTOM. Collectors' nickname for fantasy stamps, usually described as **Bogus**.

PHILATELIC HANDLING LABELS. Instructional labels provided by some postal authorities for collectors to affix to covers in order to ensure careful postmarking and handling in transit. Germany, Austria, Czechoslovakia and others have used elongated labels, part green and part white, with a double-circle emblem in the centre, and an inscription signifying "Collector Stamps - cancel carefully".

Philatelic Handling Labels—requesting postal staff to cancel mail carefully

PHONOPOSTAL STAMPS. *See* Recorded Message Stamps.

PHOSPHOR. The popular name for stamps overprinted, inked or impregnated with phosphorescent or fluorescent substances for use in electronic letter facing and cancelling machines. Such stamps on letters react or fluoresce, i.e. emit rays of a certain wavelength when subjected to radiation under ultra-violet lamps. The resulting glow of the phosphorescent ink is "seen" by the scanner, which separates first and second class mail. Phosphor bands were applied to the face of British stamps in 1959, superseding the 1957 experiment using **graphite lines**. Phosphor bands have remained in use to this day, a single band being used on the stamp denoting the basic second class rate, and two bands on some others. In 1969, however, the British Post Office began experimenting with "phosphorised paper" or "phosphor-coated paper" (PCP), first used for the 1s6d stamp and employed on many of the decimal definitives since 1976. Furthermore, to improve mechanised handling, most commemoratives from the ·1972 Silver Wedding issue to the Rowland Hill death centenary set of 1979 had "all-over phosphor" applied by the printing cylinder across the entire surface of the stamp. This was extended to the 1, 2 and 10p definitives in October 1979, as a temporary measure pending the introduction of phosphorised paper. An improved phosphorised paper called "Advanced Coated Paper" (ACP) was introduced in 1983. Similar techniques have been adopted in many other countries. *See also* Helecon, Luminescence and Tagged Stamps.   ∎

PHOSPHOR DOTS. Patterns of dots produced by phosphorescent or fluorescent substances, applied to mail to "translate" the **postcode** from an alpha-numeric sequence to a medium which can be read by sorting equipment. Trials with coding machines took place in November 1957 and led to the installation of an operational coding machine at Luton (July 1960). Since then coding patterns have gradually been extended throughout Britain as machines came into use at mechanised letter offices. The dots themselves have evolved over the years: circular, square, or rectangular, colourless with a blue, green or violet afterglow, and (since 1978) coloured blue dots. Similar devices are now used in many other countries.   ∎

PHOTOGRAPHY. As a stamp production technique, it has seldom been used. The 1d and 3d stamps issued at Mafeking during the siege of 1900 were printed by the ferroprussiate process used in reproducing draftsman's technical drawings. Other examples include the Dusitanos (Thailand) 3 satang local stamp (1910), the Regensburg air stamps (1912), the semi-official Chilean air stamp portraying Figueroa (1919) and the Mount Athos stamps prepared aboard HMS Ark Royal (1916).   ∎

PHOTOGRAVURE. Also known in the printing world simply as "gravure", in America as "rotogravure" and in France as "heliogravure". A form of intaglio printing in which the basic design is photographed and the negative used as a kind of master die from which a series of positive images to the required number for a sheet of stamps is produced on a glass plate, known as the **multipositive.** The plate is processed upon a carbon tissue which has a screened surface - a fine network of criss-cross lines. Next, the carbon tissue is wrapped around a copper cylinder and etched with a solution of ferric chloride, leaving a pattern of small cells or recesses (corresponding to the grid formation of the screen) on the cylinder. These recesses vary in depth according to the strength of tone in the multipositive images. The cylinder is then chromium-plated and prepared for printing. Photogravure was developed in Germany in the 1890s for book and magazine illustration and first used for the Bavarian definitive series printed by Bruckmann of Munich in 1914. Harrison and Sons (Egypt, 1923), Vaugirard of Paris (French colonies) and Courvoisier of La Chaux de Fonds, Switzerland, were the earliest exponents of this process on a large scale.   ■

PHOTO-LITHOGRAPHY. Otherwise known as photographic lithography, it was developed in the late 19th century for printing multicoloured labels. It was first used for postage stamps in 1911, when Oskar Consee of Munich produced the sets commemorating the 90th birthday of Prince Regent Luitpold and the 25th anniversary of his regency. Both line and multicolour half-tone photo-lithography were used in the production of West Germany's Mona Lisa stamp of 1952.

PHQ CARDS. Postcards reproducing postage stamps of commemorative and special issues, produced by the British PO since 1973. The name is derived from the initials of Postal Headquarters.

Photo-Lithography—Colourful modern issues

PHQ Card—GB 1984 Cattle stamp PHQ card used as a 'maximum card'

PICTORIAL POSTMARKS. Handstruck marks and machine impressions which include a pictorial element. The earliest marks were the heraldic types used by the Italian city states from the 15th century onwards. Other early examples include French paid marks (c. 1700) with the fleur de lis emblem, and the postmark of Leon, Spain (1750) depicting a lion. The Perth "lamb" (1750), Fort William "thistle" (1769), Birmingham "chandelier" (1772) and Dublin "mermaids" (1808–14) were the earliest from the British Isles. Between 1850 and 1880 many offices in the United States and Canada used **cork cancels** cut into fancy shapes, including numerous pictorial devices. **Special event handstamps** with a pictorial motif date from 1890 and are now extremely popular in many countries, while slogans with a pictorial device date from the 1900s. Pictorial tourist publicity slogans, notably the French **flammes illustrees**, date from 1950.

Pictorial Postmarks ancient and modern

PIGEON POST. The transmission of messages by carrier pigeon. This method was known to the Romans, but was first systematically used during the siege of Leiden (1575). The first commercial pigeon post operated between Galle and Colombo (1855–8). During the siege of Paris (1870–1) over 300 pigeons flew into the city with handwritten flimsies, and later microfilm pellicules which were transcribed and delivered to addressees. The pigeons were flown out again by manned balloon. Special stationery and stamps were first used in 1897–8 for the Great Barrier Islands pigeongram service, New Zealand. Since then there have been many services, mostly commemorative in nature, notably in India (1931–41), France, the UK and USA.

Pigeon Post—Great Barrier Island, 1897–8

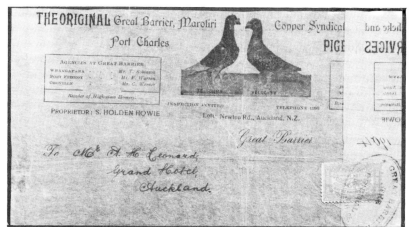

Pigeon Post—Great Barrier Island stamp used on cover

Pillars in margin of between rows of British stamps (plain margin at left)

Pin Roulette (Mexico; Kishangarh, Indian State)

PILLARS. Typeset or engraved ornament in columns of short horizontal lines, used as filling in the gutters and sheet margins of some letterpress stamps, partly to relieve the pressure on the printing plates and partly to deprive would-be forgers of blank watermarked security paper.

PIN ROULETTE. Otherwise known as *Percé en pointes*, this type of roulette consists of a series of holes pricked in the paper. Some Mexican stamps are known with a roulette produced by square pins. Most examples of pin roulette are produced by a sewing-machine in times of emergency.

PLAGIARISM. Artistic theft which, in the philatelic context, takes the form of designs originating in one country being used by another, subject only to relatively minor modifications, such as inscriptions and denominations. Good examples are the 1856 stamps of Corrientes, based on French "Ceres" stamps of 1849, the 1898 Uruguay stamp based on Newfoundland's 3c of 1890, Cretan postage due labels of 1901 based on Norway's Posthorn series, the Dominican Republic's express delivery stamp of 1925 copying the US special delivery stamp of 1922, and postage due labels of Mexico (1882), New South Wales (1891) and Australia (1902–9) copying US labels of 1879.

PLATE FLAW. Blemish on a stamp caused by damage to the printing plate. Good examples may be found on stamps of Queensland. The 2d Daniel O' Connell stamp of Ireland (1929) exhibits the famous "Screwdriver Flaw" on the 12th stamp of the 15th row, caused by a workman dropping his screwdriver on to the plate. The damage was repaired but shows as a thickening of lines in the affected part. Flaws on British Wilding definitives, such as on the numeral of the 2d and the "Butterfly flaw", may be found before and after repair, the latter being known as a **Retouch**.

Plate Flaw—constant varieties on Commonwealth stamps

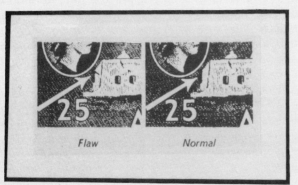

Flaw   Normal

Flaw—constant variety on Aden stamp

Flaw at right end of bar at top

White spot between 'U' and 'S' of 'MAURITIUS'

No cross on crown

White patches at left margin above value

Flaw by ear shows as an extra pearl in earring

Retouch over ear

PLATE NUMBER. Numeral, occasionally with a letter suffix, usually inscribed on the sheet margins to denote the plate from which stamps were printed. Some plates are divided into two or more panes and the latter are usually denoted by the suffix letters. Many British stamps from 1858 to 1880 bore the plate numbers within the framework of the stamps themselves, as well as in the sheet margins.

Plate Number—small number in border of GB Penny Red, larger numbers in sheet margin of Ceylon and Hong Kong stamps

PLATE PROOF. An impression taken by the plate-maker or printer from the plate, lithographic stone or etched cylinder prior to printing, to ensure that there are no flaws or errors. A careful examination of the proof will reveal whether any **retouching**, **re-engraving** or other corrections are necessary. ∎

PLEBISCITE STAMPS. Stamps issued by temporarily independent postal administrations, in towns or districts while their future nationality or political affinity is determined by a vote of the people. Plebiscites arose after the First World War, in accordance with the principle of self-determination, and stamps were issued in Allenstein, Carinthia, Eastern and Upper Silesia, Marienwerder, Memel, the Saar, Slesvig and Slovenia. Peru issued **compulsory stamps** in 1925–8 to raise money for the plebiscite in Tacna and Arica, seized by Chile in the war of 1879–85.

Plebiscite Stamps (Schleswig, Allenstein, Slovenia, Peru)

PLUG. Literally a part of a printing plate plugged into the main design. A good example is provided by the early stamps of Haiti which were all produced from the same plate, the various figures of value being plugged in as required. A similar technique is sometimes used to repair damaged plates. The term is also used by collectors to denote the loose type (more correctly "slugs") used in datestamps.

Plug (Haiti)

PNEUMATIC POST. A system of conveying letters and cards by pneumatic tubes. France established a *Reseau pneumatique* in Paris (1866), while Germany (1867) and Austria (1873) introduced a similar service, known as the *Rohrpost*. Special stationery and postmarks are known. Italy issued special stamps (1913–66) in connexion with pneumatic posts in Rome, Milan, Naples, Genoa and Turin. A pneumatic system was invented in England in 1829 and used by the Post Office for the conveyance of mailbags (1863–73).

strident nationalism of Italy and Germany are the politico-economic themes of many Soviet stamps since 1929. Stamps designed or overprinted in pursuance of territorial claims are especially popular in Latin America, and range from Venezuela's map stamps (1896) claiming British Guiana, to the Argentinian stamps (1947–83) claiming the Falkland Islands. Propaganda of a virulently anti-American character has appeared on the stamps of North Korea and North Vietnam.

Pneumatic Post stamp (Italy) and label (Bohemia and Moravia)

POACHED EGG. Collectors' nickname for a green **testing label** used by the British Post Office to check the efficiency of vending machines. Examples came into the possession of the public in mysterious circumstances, and there are even examples known to have been used postally without detection and surcharge, although such usage was never sanctioned officially.

Political Propaganda (Germany, France, Russia, Japan)

Poached Egg—nickname for GB coil testing label

POLITICAL PROPAGANDA. Postage stamps have proved a highly effective medium for the dissemination of political propaganda since the 1930s when Fascist Italy and Nazi Germany developed this usage, although there had been isolated examples from 1896 onwards. Compared with the

POLYVINYL ALCOHOL GUM. Adhesive substance which is virtually invisible and non-curling, employed on many stamps and labels since the late 1960s and usually indicated by the abbreviation PVA. British photogravure stamps adopted this gum in 1968. De La Rue use the term polyvinyl hydroxyl (PVOH) to describe the same adhesive. Gum with dextrin added is known as PVAD and has been used since 1973, bluish green colouring matter being added to distinguish it from the earlier PVA gum.

POROUS PAPER. Very soft, absorbent paper, usually unglazed.   ∎

PORTE DE MAR. Spanish meaning "carried by sea", and inscribed on Mexican stamps (1875–9) for use on seaborne European mail to indicate the fees due to be paid to the owners of the British and French mailboats employed on this service. These stamps were withdrawn from use when Mexico joined the Universal Postal Union.

POST OFFICE FORMS, STAMPS PRINTED ON. A type of **postal stationery** in which fees are denoted by means of stamps embossed or impressed on forms. This applies to many issues of telegram forms, but also to vaccination certificates, and the earliest certificates of posting for unregistered packets.

POST OFFICES ABROAD. Post offices and postal agencies staffed and operated by one country, located in another country, international zone, concession or occupied territory.

Such offices may use the ordinary stamps of the country operating the service, distinguishable only by the **cancellations**. Such stamps are described as being **Used Abroad.** Later offices of this type used stamps appropriately overprinted or inscribed, e.g. the British postal agencies in Morocco, the Gulf States, China, the Levant, Crete and Bangkok, and the issues of the French, German, Italian, Japanese, US, Russian, Austrian, Polish, Indian and Rumanian Post Offices in various parts of the world.

POST-A-BOOK. A service of the British Post Office, operated through retail bookshops as a convenient way of sending books by post. The chief interest of this service, introduced in 1983, was the use of distinctive labels, stationery and self-adhesive postage stamps similar in design to that later adopted for the **Royal Mail postage labels** of 1984–5.

Post Office Form (GB Certificate of Posting, 1878)

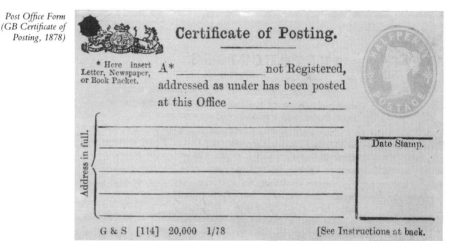

Certificate of Posting.

* Here insert Letter, Newspaper, or Book Packet.

A* _____ not Registered, addressed as under has been posted at this Office _____ .

Address in full.

Date Stamp.

G & S [114] 20,000 1/78

[See Instructions at back.

Porte de Mar

Post Offices Abroad—overprints on GB and German stamps

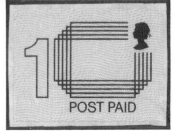

Post-a-Book Stamp—British PO service for booksellers

POSTAGE DUE LABELS. Labels, sometimes loosely described as stamps, without postal validity in themselves, but employed by many postal authorities to denote the charges to be raised from the addressees on unpaid or underpaid correspondence. They are not sold to the general public, but are usually available from philatelic counters and bureaux. Such labels were pioneered by France in 1859 but not adopted in Britain till 1914. They are also known as **To Pay labels** on account of the inscription now used by the British Post Office to encompass Customs charges as well as deficient postage. They may be recognised by such inscriptions as A PAYER, A PERCEVOIR, TAXE (French), TE BETALEN (Dutch), SEGNATASSE (Italian), PORTEADO, A COBRAR (Portuguese), MULTA, MULTADA, DEFICIT, A DEBE DEFICIENTE, DEFICIENCIA (Spanish), DOPLATIT (Czech), DOPLATA (Polish), PORTO (German), LOSEN (Swedish) or TAXA DA PLATA (Rumanian).

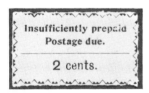

Postage Due Labels

POSTAGE CURRENCY. Name inscribed on certain issues of **Fractional currency** authorised by the US Federal Treasury during and after the American Civil War. These notes circulated in lieu of small change and were redeemable at any federal post office for postage stamps of the same value.

POSTAGE PAID IMPRESSIONS. Handstruck or printed marks applied to bulk postings of mail prepaid in cash. This system was adopted by the British Post Office in 1966 and it is now extensively used as an alternative to other forms of **bulk posting** and **metered mail**. PPIs show the serial number of the licensee, the class of posting – first or second class, rebate or parcel post – and the office of issue, although impressions intended for use at more than one office may have the designation PHQ (Postal Headquarters) instead. This system is not unlike the **Permit Mail** system in other countries.

*Postage Paid Impressions
(Rebate mail and Second Class)*

POSTAL CHARGE LABELS. Stamps thus overprinted were issued by Papua New Guinea for use as **Postage Due labels**. The term also denotes adhesive labels used by many postal administrations to indicate Customs, postal handling fees and redirectional charges due on parcels.

Postal Charge Labels (Papua-New Guinea, 1960)

Postal Fiscals (GB Inland Revenue)

POSTAL FISCALS. Stamps originally intended to denote taxes and duties and thus inscribed, but subsequently authorised to be used postally. Not to be confused with stamps inscribed "Postage and Revenue" which could be used for either purpose.

POSTAL FORGERY. A counterfeit stamp prepared specifically to defraud the postal authorities.

POSTAL FRANK. Term used rather loosely to denote accountancy labels prepared by the British Vice-Consulate in Antananarivo, Madagascar and sold to local residents and businessmen to facilitate handling of mail through the Consular post. These franks were attached to letters by one corner only, so that they could be easily detached at the Consulate before the letters were forwarded to the postmaster at Port Louis, where they were franked with appropriate postage stamps of Mauritius or Reunion and the amount debited to the Consulate in Antananarivo. They were therefore not postage stamps in the usual sense, although they denoted the prepayment of postage.

POSTAL HISTORY. The study of the origins and development of postal services and all aspects pertaining to them. Branches of postal history which now have their own specialist societies include airmails, travelling post offices and even mailboxes. The term is also applied very loosely to collectable material, such as **postmarks**, **postal stationery** and stamped covers and cards.

Postal Franks (Madagascar, 1896)

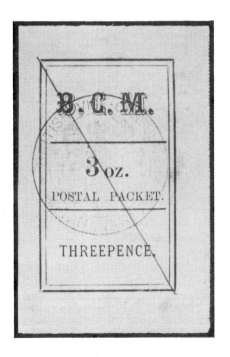

Postal History—interesting postal markings on reply postcard from Argentina to the Falkland Islands

Postal Markings on postal service cover from 'Department of Posts, Turkish Republic of Northern Cyprus'

Postal Mechanisation— Canadian and GB covers showing postcode markings

POSTAL MARKING. Any kind of mark applied to a postal packet in connexion with its transmission by post. The term is used to include both manuscript endorsement and handstruck or machine postmarks, accountancy marks, route marks and **cachets**.

POSTAL MECHANISATION. The study of the development of postal handling by mechanical and electronic means, usually exemplified by the collecting of items which have passed through automatic sorting equipment or postcode machinery, the postmarks applied by facer-canceller tables (FCT), **Transorma** markings, ident codes and **phosphor dots**, and the ephemera associated with the publicity campaign to encourage more widespread use of **postcodes** and **Zip Codes**.

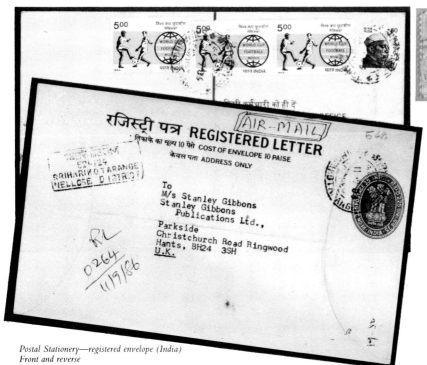

Postal Stationery—registered envelope (India)
Front and reverse

Postal Telegraphs (Argentina, Chile, Western Australia)

POSTAL SEAL. Circular label used to seal the flaps of official covers and signify offical mail exempt from postal charges. The best-known examples of these are the **Interpostal seals** used by the Egyptian Post Office, but they were also widely used in Austria and the German Empire up to the First World War. *See also* Sealing Labels.

POSTAL STATIONERY. All kinds of **envelopes**, **letter sheets**, **letter-cards**, **postcards**, **wrappers**, **aerogrammes** which, because of their inscriptions or the stamps embossed or impressed thereon, are entitled to pass through the post without extra charge. Traditionally such stationery was recognised by having imprinted stamps, but it should be noted that the **Mulready** stationery did not come into that category, and this definition excluded many classes of stationery designed for official use. In recent times, moreover, there has been a tendency to avoid the use of imprinted stamps of fixed value, and substitute a device merely indicating that postage has been prepaid, e.g. British **postnotes** (1982), 1st and 2nd class envelopes (1984), aerogrammes and registered envelopes (1986).

POSTAL TELEGRAPHS. Stamps originally issued for use on telegrams but subsequently permitted, provisionally or permanently, for use as postage stamps. Unless this change of status is indicated by means of an overprint, postal usage can only be detected by the type of cancellation employed. As many telegraphic cancellations are the same as, or very similar to, postmarks, it is often impossible to distinguish actual usage unless the stamps are still attached to the original cover, card or form. Conversely many higher-value postage stamps were intended primarily for telegraphic usage. Many GB shilling stamps of the 1880s, for example, with single-circle cancellations, would have been used telegraphically.

POSTAL UNION COLOURS. The Universal Postal Union, almost from its inception, urged member countries to adopt certain colours for the stamps used in overseas mail, and it was for this reason that the GB twopence halfpenny changed from rosy mauve to blue in 1880 to denote the foreign letter rate. This recommendation became mandatory as a result of the Postal Union Congress in Washington (1898). The colours green, red and blue were recommended for the stamps prepaying the basic foreign printed matter, postcard and single-rate letters respectively. These colours fell into disuse as the result of inflation and the disparity of postal rates following the Second World War, and the scheme was finally abandoned in 1953. ∎

Postbus Ticket (Hailsham-Bodle Street Green service, 1974)

Postcard (Sri Lanka)

POSTBUS TICKET. Many of the postbus services which have operated in the UK since 1967 use distinctive tickets which are of considerable interest to postal historians. Other tickets, however, have their value denoted by means of adhesive postage stamps which require cancellation, and for this purpose rubber stamps, often in the outline of a postbus, are employed. These tickets therefore possess interest for philatelists as well as postal historians.

POSTCARD. A type of postal stationery, consisting of small sheets of pasteboard or cardboard, generally transmitted by post at much lower rates than letter mail. It was invented by Dr Emmanuel Herrmann of Vienna and adopted by the Austro-Hungarian postal administration in 1869 and by other countries, including Britain, a year later. Picture postcards developed in Europe in the 1880s but were not permitted in Britain till 1894.

POSTCARD STAMP. An adhesive postage stamp overprinted for use on postcards issued by the Orange Free State, 1889–97. Stamps of various denominations, denoting internal, South African and overseas postage, were affixed to the cards and then overprinted with the national coat of arms.

Postcard Stamp (Orange Free State)

POSTCARD TAX STAMPS. Persian stamps overprinted "Controle" and issued in 1904 to denote a tax on picture postcards sent through the post. They had to be affixed to cards in addition to the normal postage.

POSTCODE. A group of numbers, or combination of letters and numbers, devised to translate an address into a code which can be used by automatic sorting equipment. Germany pioneered two-digit (1942) and four-digit (1961) codes, which were subsequently adopted by Switzerland (1964), Austria (1966), Australia and Denmark (1967), Norway (1968) and Belgium (1969). Five-figure codes were adopted by the USA (1963), France (1965), Italy (1967), Sweden (1968) and both Finland and Yugoslavia (1971). Japan adopted a variable three to five-digit code in 1968. These numerical groups only gave outward coding, and are not as sophisticated as the alphanumeric system pioneered by Britain (1959–73). The Philippines (1968) and Canada (1971–4) are other countries using this system to denote inward and outward codes. Apart from the effect of postcoding on mail, notably in the use of **phosphor dots** and other electronic markings, the campaign urging the public to use postcodes has resulted in numerous slogan postmarks, stamps, labels and ephemera. *See also* Zip Code.

POSTMARK. Any mark, in manuscript, applied by handstamp, or by machine, connected with the postal service and found on matter transmitted by post. Postmarks therefore include **cancellations** of all kinds which are designed to cancel or obliterate postage stamps in order to prevent their re-use. Postmarks in general may have the function of identifying the office of collection or delivery, the date on which the item was handled, or some instruction regarding special handling. Postmarks denoting the prepayment of postage in cash may be regarded as a form of postage stamp, either handstruck or applied by machine. In theory they also include everything from **slogan postmarks** to **charge** and **explanatory marks**, from **meter marks** to **postage paid impressions**. The earliest postal markings of any kind were the red and blue marks on Egyptian letters, c. 3000 BC, bearing an exhortation in the name of the Pharaoh. The earliest in Europe were manuscript markings on Venetian letters of the 13th century. Manuscript postal charges date from the mid-16th century (France) and handstruck postmarks from the early 14th century (Milan). *See also* Advertisement Postmarks, Backstamp, Bar Cancel, Blackout Cancel, Cancellation, Circular Datestamp, Climax Dater, Coloured Postmarks, Commatology, Commemorative Postmarks, Cork Cancels, Datestamps, Double Stamp, Dumb Cancellation, Duplex, Flag Cancel, Flammes Illustrees, Handstruck Postage Stamps, Late Fee Postmarks, Machine Cancellation, Manuscript Cancellation, Multilingual Postmarks, Obliteration, Paid, Parcel Postmark, Pen Cancelled, Pictorial Postmarks, Postage Paid Impressions, Private Postmarks, Publicity Slogan, Relief Cancel, Skeleton Handstamp, Slogan Postmark, Spoon Cancellation, Squared Circle and Temporary Rubber Datestamp.

Postcard Tax Stamps (Persia, 1904)

Postcode—GB label for use on letterheads

Postmark—USA Boston General Mail Facility

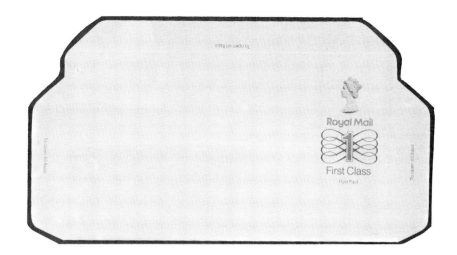

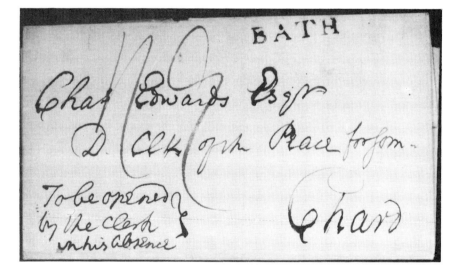

(above) *Postmasters' Stamps (New York; Alexandria, 1845–6)*

(above right) *Postnote— new form of British postal stationery (1982)*

(right) *Pre-adhesive cover sent from Bath to Chard*

POSTMASTERS' STAMPS. Postage stamps issued by the postmasters of certain towns and cities in the United States, Canada and Bermuda to facilitate the prepayment of postage, prior to the introduction of government issues. The term is also applied to stamps issued on the authority of individual postmasters in times of political and economic upheaval, e.g. the American Civil War and in Germany at the end of the Second World War.

POSTNOTE. Term devised by the British Post Office to describe a type of postal stationery introduced in 1982, not unlike an **aerogramme** but printed on thicker paper and intended for internal first class mail. The impressed stamp was **undenominated**, so that postnotes could be sold at a variable price, according to the prevailing first class rate.

PRE-ADHESIVE. Used to describe a piece of mail which has been transmitted by post before the advent of adhesive stamps in the country of origin. Sometimes the term "pre-stamp" is erroneously used in this context, ignoring the existence of handstruck postage stamps before adhesive stamps were introduced.

*Pre-Cancel used by
Stamford Mercury
newspaper*

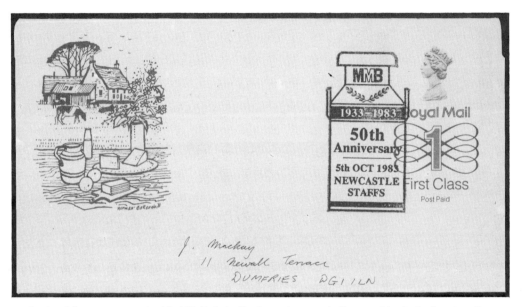

Premium Offers—postnote overprinted for Milk Marketing Board promotion; stamp booklet cover giving details of premium offer

PRE-CANCEL. Alternatively known as a pre-cancelled stamp, this is a postage stamp intended for use by bulk posters and bearing a form of handstruck or machine-printed cancellation. Although the stamps are usually adhesive, it should be noted that both postal stationery and impressed newspaper stamps are known to have been pre-cancelled. This system was used in Britain for newspapers and printed matter from 1870 onwards, but is best known in connexion with stamps of Canada and the USA (overprinted with town names or licence numbers between horizontal bars), or France (AFFRANCHts). Various forms of pre-cancellation have also been practised in Belgium and Luxembourg.

PREMIÈRES GRAVURES. French for "first engravings",

the term used to describe the original version of the US 1861 series, the designs being subsequently altered in subtle ways.

■

PREMIUM OFFERS. Goods or services offered free or at a discount as a sales incentive. In the postal context it describes sales promotions which offer stamps or postal stationery in exchange for wrappers or tops collected from certain branded goods. Several offers of this sort have been made in Britain in recent years, notably the Dairy **postnotes** in connexion with a dairy product offer. The Post Office also used stamp booklets to promote the "Write Now" letter-pack, writing sets, greetings cards and even recorded message cassettes. The lastname involved the use of self-adhesive stamps, similar to the **Royal Mail postage labels**.

PRESENTATION PACK. A philatelic souvenir containing a set of stamps and some form of descriptive text. Packs were first issued by the British Post Office in April 1964 (Shakespeare series). Later this medium was extended to regional and unified definitive stamps and postage due labels. Many other postal administrations now offer such packs, for individual issues as well as entire year collections.

PRESTIGE BOOKLET. A stamp booklet which is not only sponsored by a particular company or organisation but contains special panes of stamps with descriptive text printed alongside. These booklets originated in 1969 in a £1 booklet entitled "Stamps for Cooks", issued by the British Post Office. Subsequently high-value booklets have been sponsored by Wedgwood (1972 and 1980), Stanley Gibbons (1982), the Royal Mint (1983), Christian Heritage (1984), *The Times* (1985), British Rail (1986) and P & O Shipping (1987). A feature of these booklets is their large-sized panes which invariably include one or more stamps with phosphor band variants not found on sheet stamps.

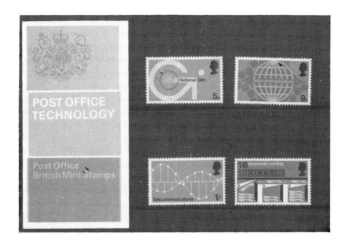

Presentation Pack (GB Post Office Technology issue, 1969)

Prestige Booklet—GB 1972 Story of Wedgwood

PRINTED MATTER. Circulars, samples and other forms of commercial papers, transmitted through the post at reduced rates of postage. Distinctive stamps, stationery and postmarks have been produced in many countries in connexion with this class of mail. Stamps inscribed IMPRESOS were first issued by the Philippines (1886) and Cuba (1888). Czechoslovakia overprinted stamps O.T. (*Obchodni Tiskopis* = commercial printed matter) in 1934 and stamps of Bohemia and Moravia were overprinted GD-OT in 1940 for the same purpose (*Geschäfts Drucksache*). US stamps in very low or fractional denominations, with or without pre-cancels or inscriptions indicating **bulk rate** or **authorised non-profit organisations** also come into this category.

Printed Matter (Spanish Philippines, Czechoslovakia)

PRINTED ON BACK. Numerous stamps may be found with some form of printing on the back: Greek stamps with the denomination on the reverse (1861–80), British stamps with the names of organisations or firms as a security measure (1867–82), Swedish stamps with a blue posthorn (1886–91), advertisements on the back of British (1887) and New Zealand (1893) stamps, serial number on the stamps of Spain and colonies, **coils** of France and Germany with control numbers on certain stamps, **burélé** pattern on Queensland stamps and **graphite lines** on British stamps (1957). Portugal pioneered inscriptions on the back of commemorative stamps (1895), the St Anthony series bearing the text of his prayer on the reverse. In more recent years stamps of this type have been issued by Hungary (1925), Gibraltar (1969–76), Portugal (1968–71), Mauritius (1971) and the USA (1973). British stamps with a letter D or a five-pointed star on the reverse come from **discount** booklets. *See also* Adson, Underprint.

PRINTED WATERMARK. Imitation watermark adopted either as a cheap substitute for security paper during a temporary shortage, or as an experimental measure. Stamps with simulated watermarks, printed on the back have been issued by Argentina (1922), El Salvador (1935) and New Zealand (1925).

Printed Watermark (New Zealand 1925, 'NZ and Star' applied by lithovarnish)

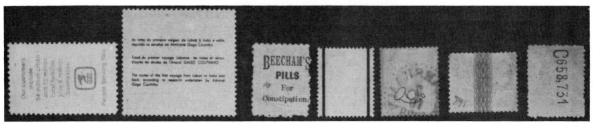

Printed on Back

PRINTER'S ORNAMENT AND RULE. Decorative elements used in typography to break up blocks of text. They have been used in the production of **typeset stamps** to provide ornamental framework, and also in the setting of overprints, various ornamental devices being used to blot out original values.

Printer's Ornament and Rule (Madagascar)

PRINTER'S WASTE. Any defective, malformed or misprinted stamps which are normally scrapped and destroyed by the printer, but which have been known to leak on to the philatelic market. ■

PRISONER OF WAR MAIL. Correspondence to or from prisoners of war is recorded from the Napoleonic period onwards, distinguished by special postmarks, camp **cachets** and **censor marks**. Special stationery for this purpose was first used during the First World War, while Britain and New Zealand produced distinctive aerogrammes for mail to servicemen in Italian, German and Japanese camps during the Second World War. Stamps printed by the inmates of internment camps were produced during the First World War, but numerous issues were made by Polish prisoners at Murnau, Grossborn, Neubrandenburg and Woldenburg during the Second World War. *See also* Internee mail.

PRIVATE CONTROLS. Inscriptions overprinted or underprinted on stamps used by firms, institutions and organisations to prevent pilferage or improper use by their staff. *See also* Perfins.

Private Controls

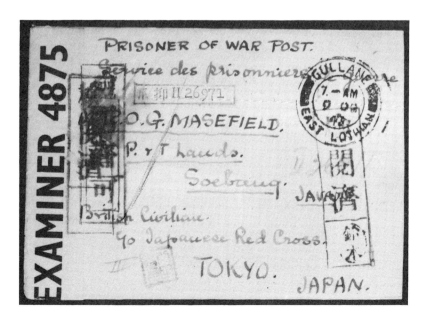

Prisoner of War stamp and cover

PRIVATE LABELS. Labels without postal validity, affixed to cards and covers to advertise companies and their products, hotels, tourist resorts, special events or commercial propaganda. *See also* Charity, Commemorative and Exhibition labels.

Private Labels—advertising Tenby and the Hyde Park Hotel

PRIVATE PERFORATION. Unofficial perforation applied by private individuals or organisations before perforation methods were generally adopted. Susse Freres of Paris perforated the current French stamps of 1861, making large holes gauging about 7, while Greek stamps of 1889–95 may be found perforated 8.5 × 9.25 by the postmaster at Astakos, or pinrouletted by the postmaster at Amphissa. Many US coil stamps were privately perforated for use in firms' dispensing machines.

Private Perforation (Greece, France)

PRIVATE POSTMARKS. Rotary or machine cancellations permitted in the USA, West Germany and Belgium for the use of firms and organisations. These postmarks resemble ordinary slogan cancellations in many respects, but incorporate firms' advertisements and usually a licence number. They are used extensively on mail-shots bearing adhesive stamps, as a more readily acceptable alternative to **metered mail** or **postage paid impressions**. The British Post Office sanctioned the use of private postmarks by several newspapers, the last to make use of this facility being the *Stamford Mercury* in the 1960s. Several stationers, such as W.H. Smith, Smith, Elder & Co., William Dawson & Sons and H.S. King & Co., used their own distinctive postmarks from 1865 onwards.

Private Postmark (West Germany)

PRIVATE STAMPS. An alternative term for Franchise stamps.

PRIVILEGE ENVELOPE. Envelope giving preferential postal treatment to a charitable organisation. They were first issued by Prussia in 1867 for use by the Crown Princess Victoria National Invalids' Foundation for wounded soldiers after the Seven Weeks' War with Austria. Packets were transmitted at a flat rate of 4pf irrespective of weight or size. Special postmarks inscribed CHARITY LETTER were used in England in the early 19th century and served a similar purpose.

PRO AERO. Inscription or overprint on certain air stamps of Switzerland, provided in connexion with special flights between 1938 and 1949. The first of these was not sold to the public, but affixed to **first flight covers** by postal officials. It is thus extremely rare in mint condition.

Pro Aero—stamp for Swiss special flight

PRO JUVENTUTE. Latin meaning "on behalf of youth", inscribed on Swiss stamps since 1913 issued for children's charities.

Pro Juventute (Switzerland, 1963)

PRO PATRIA. Latin meaning "For the Fatherland", inscribed on Swiss stamps issued from 1952 onwards with a charity premium in aid of national culture funds.

Pro Patria (Switzerland, 1981)

PROOF. Impression taken during the preparation of the master die or printing plate prior to the manufacture of postage stamps. The various types are described under Colour Proof, Die Proof, Engraver's Progress Proof and Used Proof.

PROPAGANDA FORGERIES. Stamps forged by British Intelligence during both world wars and smuggled into enemy territory to be used by Allied agents to frank propaganda leaflets. Stamps have also been forged with their designs satirically distorted for propaganda purposes. These were not intended to frank mail and may therefore be regarded more correctly as propaganda labels.

Propaganda Forgery (Bavaria, First World War)

PROPAGANDA LEAFLETS. Leaflets bearing propaganda messages aimed at enemy forces or population have been an important aspect of psychological warfare since the early 19th century, propelled by artillery shells or dropped by balloons and aircraft. This technique was widely used by both sides during the Second World War and in subsequent campaigns and periods of civil unrest.

PROPAGANDA STAMPS. Stamps designed to promote campaigns and get a message across to the public. Italy (1954–5) and Venezuela (1974) have issued stamps urging their citizens to pay their taxes promptly. In recent years many countries have issued stamps urging road safety, food production, family planning, anti-pollution, anti-smoking, the prevention of drug abuse and accident prevention.

Propaganda Stamps

PROVISIONAL LABELS. Parcel and **Registration labels**, were normally issued with inscriptions distinctive to each post office, but provisional types were produced by handstamping or manuscript endorsement, either during temporary shortages or to meet special purposes, e.g. at fairs, exhibitions and sporting events.

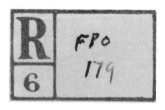

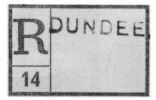

Provisional Stamps

Provisional Labels (Registration)

PUBLICITY ENVELOPE STAMPS. Italian definitive stamps overprinted B.L.P. (*Buste Lettere Postali*) and issued in 1921–3. They were sold at a discount of 5 per cent to an exservicemen's society and were affixed to envelopes or lettercards bearing advertisements, the project being designed to assist disabled veterans.

PROVISIONAL STAMPS. Stamps whose value or purpose has been altered after printing, by means of a **surcharge** or **overprint**. The earliest instance occurred in 1854 when Mauritius issued undenominated stamps overprinted FOURPENCE. In 1855 Cuba and Porto Rico issued provisionals surcharged with new values. Thereafter this practice was widely resorted to, usually during emergencies and temporary shortages.

Publicity Slogan Postmark (Hastings, 1963)

PUBLICITY SLOGAN POSTMARK. A type of machine cancellation intended to publicise the industry or tourist potential of a town or district. The first local publicity slogans were used in France in the early 1920s at holiday resorts. They were non-pictorial until 1950 when the first **flammes illustrees** were introduced. Publicity slogans spread to the USA (1921) and were subsequently used in Canada, New Zealand, Belgium, Switzerland and Ireland before the Second World War. The first British slogans of this type were used in 1963.

QUADRILLE PAPER. Paper watermarked with crossed lines forming a pattern of small squares. A rectangular pattern is described as "oblong quadrille", and some stamps, though described as being on quadrille paper, merely have a protective coating in such a pattern, called "surface quadrille". The term "quadrille" is also used to denote the pattern of small feint squares printed on album pages.

QUARTER. A fourth part of a divisible stamp as issued by Mecklenburg-Schwerin (1856) and Brunswick (1857). Brunswick's stamps had an individual value of a quarter gutegroschen (3pf) which prepaid the lowest postal rate (i.e. local printed matter), while the whole stamp had a value of 1 gutegroschen or 12pf.

Quarter stamps from Brunswick (1857)

Quadrille Paper (Guadalajara, Mexico; Obock; Ecuador)

QUADRIPARTITE LABELS. Postal labels consisting of four parts, divided by **roulette** or **perforation**. The best example of this is provided by the Chinese express labels of 1909, the outer portions of which served as sender's and recipient's receipts.

QUARTZ LAMP. An electric lamp incorporating a filament in transparent fused quartz, emitting and passing the maximum of ultra-violet rays, which on striking certain substances cause **fluorescence**. It is an invaluable tool of the philatelist in examining stamps for any kind of repair or tampering which would result in a fake. It is also extremely useful in identifying **aniline inks** and the different kinds of coating found in many modern stamps.

Quadripartite Labels (China, 1909)

Railway Air Services stamp (GWR, 1933)

Railway Company Stamps

RAILWAY AIR SERVICES. Airmail services operated by and on behalf of railway companies. The Great Western Railway (1933) issued its own stamps for this purpose. In 1934 the four major rail companies of the UK formed the Railway Air Service and organised an airmail network throughout the country. No stamps were issued, but distinctive handstamps and souvenir **first flight covers** are known.

RAILWAY COMPANY STAMPS. Local or semi-official stamps issued by railway companies in many countries, mainly to denote fees payable in respect of parcels, but in some cases extending to letters as well. The earliest railway stamps were issued in England (1846) for parcels, but between 1891 and 1922 many British companies issued stamps to cover a special **railway letter fee**. In Belgium and France, however, parcel stamps have been issued by the postal administrations on behalf of the state railways, while Bavarian stamps overprinted E (Eisenbahn) served the same purpose. Since 1929 Belgium has also issued special stamps for use on railway official correspondence, depicting a winged wheel emblem or a B in an oval frame, overprinted or incorporated in the design.

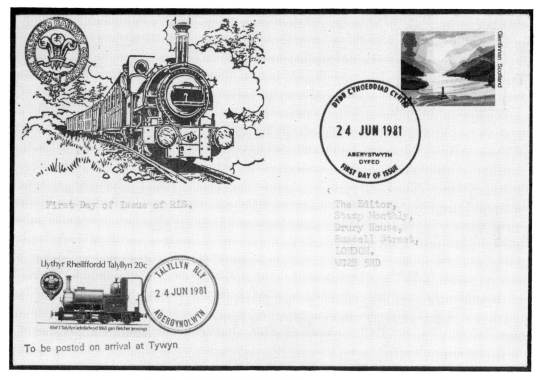

*Railway Letter Fee
stamps—1891 design and
modern issue of Talyllyn
Railway (Wales)*

RAILWAY LETTER FEE. An additional fee levied on letters handed in at stations for conveyance by passenger train, to be collected on arrival or put into the local postal delivery at the station nearest to the addressee. This service was negotiated as part of the deal whereby the British Post Office instituted an **express** service. The railways were permitted to operate their own service, provided that the letters they handled bore a penny stamp representing the ordinary inland letter rate at the time. The major companies produced 2d stamps, most of which were in a uniform green design. These stamps were phased out in 1922 when the companies were amalgamated.

Thereafter **railway parcel stamps** were used instead. In 1957, however, the private Talyllyn light railway revived the custom of issuing railway letter stamps and this has since been followed by other private light railways.

RAILWAY PARCEL STAMPS. Stamps issued by railway companies to prepay the freight charges on parcels which were permitted as they did not infringe the Postmaster-General's monopoly. Special stamps for this purpose were first issued in 1846 by the London and North Western Railway and subsequently by about 100 other companies in the British Isles alone.

Many companies issued special stamps for such diverse purposes as corn samples, market baskets, periodicals and farm produce. Many of these stamps were beautifully engraved and incorporated pictorial motifs. From 1923 onwards, however, the parcel stamps issued by the four major railway groups were more utilitarian in style, leading to the severely functional types used by British Rail which were produced by machines not unlike modern **automatic stamps**. Railway Parcel stamps were also issued by many other countries, the issues of New Zealand and the Australian states being the most notable.

READERS' DIGEST COILS. Multi-value strips of stamps produced by the British Post Office on behalf of the *Readers' Digest* and issued since September 1981, to facilitate reply postage. These coil strips subsequently became available from the British Philatelic Bureau, but specialists prefer to collect them with the appropriate mail-order cards.

Readers' Digest Coil strip (1984)

Railway Parcel Stamps (GB, Australia)

Receipted Parcels—British Post Office label

RAINBOW TRIALS. A series of **colour trials** produced by the British authorities between May and December 1840, and in March - May 1841, to test various coloured inks, cancellations and paper. The stamps were in the design of the Penny Black but were distinguished by having the top right-hand corners void and also omitting **check letters** in the lower corners. ■

RECEIPTED PARCELS. A parcel service operated by the British Post Office analogous to the **Recorded Delivery** system pertaining to letter packets. Distinctive serial labels, printed in red on yellow paper, were used in this connexion. The service has now been superseded by **Trakback**.

RECESS PRINTING. *See* Intaglio and Line Engraving.

RECORDED DELIVERY. A service of the British Post Office, similar to the **Certified Mail** system used in the United States and Australia. A receipt is given to the sender and taken from the recipient on delivery, but there is no special handling in transit. The service is used as a cheap alternative to registration. It was introduced in the UK in 1961 and has since used a wide range of distinctive labels. Special versions have been produced for **official mail** and bilingual labels for use in Wales.

Recorded Delivery—several variations of the label exist

RECORDED MESSAGE STAMPS. Stamps issued by Argentina (1939) to prepay the fees on messages recorded on discs for transmission by post, and inscribed CORREOS FONOPOSTAL. Other countries, including the UK, Irish Republic and Taiwan, have operated similar services and used distinctive postmarks and stationery, but have not issued special stamps for the purpose.

Recorded Message Stamp (Argentina, 1939)

REDRAWN. A new printing of a stamp whose design differs in some detail from the original, while retaining its principal features. Examples are the Russian "Arms" types of 1883–8, reissued with thunderbolts added to the posthorns (1889–94); and the current GB Machin decimal definitive stamps which replaced similar stamps denominated in shillings and pence. Other notable GB examples include the 2d blue without lines (1840) and with lines (1841), and the 1d lilac 14 pearls (1881) or 16 pearls (1881–1902).

Redrawn (GB Penny Lilac—14 and 16 corner pearls, Japan 'Noh Mask' original and redrawn)

RE-ENGRAVING. The strengthening of worn parts of the surface of a printing plate by hand-work, sometimes referred to as recutting. These terms are also used when an original die is deepened, prior to preparing a new plate. ∎

RE-ENTRY. Duplication of part of a line-engraved stamp design due to a first impression having been inadequately **erased**, and thus permitting traces of its entry to appear in conjunction with the new impression, causing a doubling of a part of the image. The term is also sometimes applied to the **lithographic** process, but in this case is more correctly called a double transfer.

Re-entry-Peru 1s. of 1886 showing whole stamp double (left) and normal (right)

Regional Postcard—issued by London Postal Region (1983)

Regional Stamps—Guernsey, Jersey, Isle of Man, N. Ireland, Scotland, Wales

REGIONAL POSTCARDS. Picture postcards issued by the various regional postal boards in the UK from 1971 until 1986. Normally they featured buildings or items of interest to stamp collectors and postal historians.

REGIONAL STAMPS. Postage stamps issued by the British PO since 1958 for use in Scotland, Wales, Northern Ireland, Guernsey, Jersey and the Isle of Man. These stamps were superseded by the issues of the independent postal administrations in Guernsey and Jersey (1969) and the Isle of Man (1973). They were intended to appease regional sentiment. They are fully valid for postage from any part of the UK, although normally sold only within their respective regions.

REGISTERED ENVELOPES. Special envelopes, pioneered by Britain in 1878, for registered packets and distinguished by crossed blue lines. Stout envelopes of this type, usually printed on linen-backed paper, are used by most countries and form an important class of **postal stationery**.

Registered Envelope with adhesives affixed
(Bahrain)

Registration Labels

Registered Postmark (GB, oval shape)

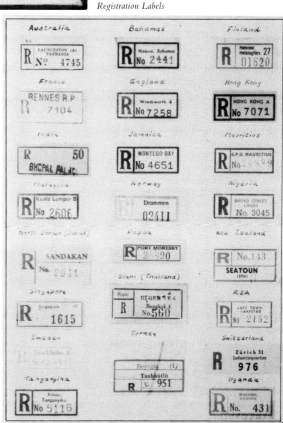

REGISTERED POSTMARKS. Special marks applied to registered packets to indicate greater security in transit. They were used in Ireland (1809–31) and throughout the UK from 1841 onwards, the distinctive oval type now current being adopted in 1853. Special marks with a crown over the word REGISTERED were applied to colonial and foreign registered packets from the early 19th century. Similar marks, inscribed RECOMMANDE, RACCOMANDATA or EINSCHREI-BEN, in French, Italian and German respectively, have been used in other countries.

REGISTRATION LABELS. Adhesive labels, usually bearing the serial number of a registered packet, affixed to such mail to distinguish it from ordinary mail and also to facilitate the hand-to-hand check in transit. The earliest labels were used in Germany and Scandinavia in the 1870s. Labels of a uniform style, incorporating a prominent R, were adopted by the

Universal Postal Union in 1882, but their use was optional and it was not until 1907 that they were introduced in Britain. Until 1973–4 every post office in the UK had its own distinctive labels, a practice which survives in many other countries, resulting in an infinite range of collectable material. As Persian postmasters had to account for their labels at the rate of 1 chahi each, they were sometimes used as postage stamps of that denomination, or combined with other stamps to make up rates. Registration labels of German New Guinea were overprinted and surcharged for temporary use as postage stamps, following the occupation of the colony by British imperial forces in 1914. Registration labels of the Austro-Hungarian Empire can be collected in matched pairs with labels from the same post offices under the various successor states, (Czechoslovakia, Yugoslavia, Poland), or re-assigned to Italy or Rumania after the First World War.

REGISTRATION STAMPS. Special stamps, adhesive or impressed on stationery, denoting the registration fee and often incorporating the ordinary postage charge as well. In some cases the stamps doubled as **registration labels** and incorporated the serial number of the packet.

*Registration Stamp
(Colombia)*

REGUMMED. Unused stamps which have lost their original gum and have had fresh adhesive added in order to pass them off as **mint** stamps – a form of **fake**.

RE-ISSUES. Stamps which have been withdrawn from use, but which are subsequently brought back into use, either from old stocks or by fresh printings from the original plates. In some cases, notably in Latin America, postal validity is renewed or confirmed by an overprint such as HABILITADO or RESELLADA. Not to be confused with new printings of current stamps, or reprints.

Re-issues (Bolivia, Newfoundland, Mexico)

RELIEF CANCEL. *See* Skeleton.

RELIGIOUS PROPAGANDA. Stamps have been used as a medium for disseminating religious messages. Notable early examples of this have included Portugal's series of 1895 commemorating St Anthony of Padua, with his prayer printed on the back, and Italy's sets publicising the Propagation of the Faith (1923) and St Francis of Assisi (1926). Many countries have issued stamps since 1924 to mark Holy Year or the international Eucharistic Congresses. Many stamps from the Vatican (since 1929) and Israel (since 1948) have publicised Catholicism and Judaism respectively, while Islamic fundamentalism has been a significant feature of many stamps from the Arab countries and Iran in recent years. *See also* Christmas seals and stamps.

Religious Propaganda

Remainders (Labuan, Trinidad, Mexico, Costa Rica)

REMAINDERS. Unsold stamps on hand after an issue has been taken off sale. Such stamps are normally destroyed, but sometimes they are overprinted, surcharged or revalidated for postage. In some cases, however. remainders have been sold to dealers and collectors, either in unused state (when they are indistinguishable from the original issue), or cancelled by some special device such as **bars**, or overprinted in some way to denote that they have been withdrawn from use, e.g. the AUSSER KURS found on obsolete Swiss stamps. Sometimes remainders are **cancelled to order** and sold off cheaply in that condition.

REPAIRED PAPER. Paper, usually from the beginning or end of reels used in rotary printing, which has been joined up by the pressman and is therefore distinguished by overlapping to some extent. Stamps printed from repaired paper show double thickness of paper in all or part of their surface area.

REPLY PAID STATIONERY. Envelopes, postcards and parcel labels bearing special inscriptions, addresses and licence numbers to enable firms' customers to reply without paying the postage. Firms and organisations using this service pay the postage and a small handling fee. A similar service is also offered by the British Post Office under the name of Freepost.

Postage
will be paid
by licensee

Do not affix postage Stamps if posted in Gt. Britain,
Channel Islands, N. Ireland or the Isle of Man

BR Licence No BH382

STANLEY GIBBONS PUBLICATIONS
Parkside, Christchurch Road,
RINGWOOD, Hampshire,
BH24 3SH.

2

Reply Paid Stationery—postage paid by recipient

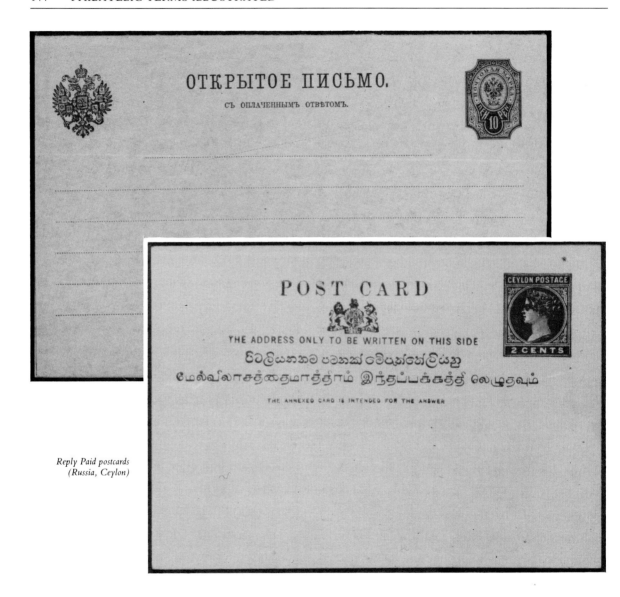

Reply Paid postcards (Russia, Ceylon)

REPLY POSTCARDS. A form of postal stationery consisting of two postcards joined together, one of the message sent originally and the other for a reply from the recipient. These cards were pioneered by Bavaria and the German Imperial Post in 1872. Britain issued such cards from 1882 till 1970.

REPP PAPER. A ribbed paper, not unlike **laid paper** but with the fine ribbing on the surface and not resulting from the watermark. Such paper has a slightly corrugated appearance, caused by milling or ridging between steel rollers during the manufacturing process. ∎

REPRINTS. Stamps other than **re-issues**, printed from the original plates after the stamps have ceased to be current. Such stamps are usually produced to satisfy philatelic demands. Sometimes the plates are disposed of by the postal administration, thus enabling private individuals to produce reprints. These may be indistinguishable from the originals, if the same paper, gum and ink are employed; but they can be differentiated and thus correctly categorised if one or more of these criteria differ from the originals. The most notorious reprints are those of certain Latin American countries' stamps, produced by Nicholas Seebeck who acquired the plates as part of his contract to supply these countries with new issues each year free of charge.

Reprints (South Australia, Nicaragua, Austria, Victoria)

RESINISED PAPER. *See* Goldbeater's Skin.

RETOUCH. A minor correction effected by hand-engraving on the plate or cylinder. The term is now commonly applied to flaws rectified on photogravure stamps.

Retouch (GB Two Pence Blue; Switzerland 'Standing Helvetia')

RETURNED LETTER STAMPS. Stamps inscribed RETOURBRIEF were issued by Bavaria and Norway for use on undeliverable mail, returned to the sender without attracting any further postal charges. There are many different types, some bearing the names of the principal offices. Although not postage stamps in the strict sense they are of considerable interest to collectors and are fully listed in some European specialised catalogues.

Returned Letter Stamp (Bavaria)

RETURNED MAIL. Correspondence and parcels returned to the sender as undeliverable for a variety of reasons, usually indicated by means of **cachets**, **postmarks** and/or **labels**. Many countries also used special envelopes, both ordinary and registered, for returning letters which have had to be opened to ascertain the name and address of the sender. The British Post Office also has special labels for the return to senders of parcels without any further charge. These are inscribed "To be delivered free" and it has therefore been argued that they constitute a form of postage stamp or **frank**. *See also* Undeliverable mail.

REVALIDATED STAMPS. *See* Re-issues.

REVENUE STAMPS. *See* Fiscal Stamps.

REVERSED PRINT. Stamps printed in reverse, by accident or design, also known as mirror prints, because of their visual effect. The 10 and 30 silbergroschen stamps of Prussia (1866) were deliberately printed in reverse on the back of transparent **goldbeater's skin**, allowing the design to show through the front. In lithography a reversed transfer, and in photogravure a reversed negative, would result in a mirror print. The same effect may be caused accidentally by a sheet of stamps, newly printed and still wet, adhering to the back of another sheet. The resulting reversed image on the back of the sheet is known as a set-off.

RIBBED PAPER. *See* Repp Paper.

RICE PAPER. A thin and delicate paper in a variety of textures, made from the sliced pith of a Formosan tree (*Fatsia papyrifera*), or from other plants or linen trimmings, and sized with rice-water. El Salvador's 1c stamp of 1889 is the only postage stamp recorded as printed on rice paper, although local stamps of Formosa are known to have been printed on the local product. ∎

ROCKET MAIL. Mail conveyed by rocket dates back to 1928 when Friedrich Schmiedl organised the first experiment in Austria. Britain's first rocket mail was staged at Rottingdean in 1934 by Gerhard Zucker who subsequently conducted experiments at Scarp (Harris) and the Solent the same year. Souvenir stamps, flimsies, cards and postmarks have been produced in connexion with rocket mails, mostly of a private or semi-official nature. Cuba (1939) issued the first official rocket stamp. Since the Apollo 11 moon-shot of 1969 there have been several instances of mail being conveyed by spacecraft, notably souvenir cards bearing the US $9.35 (1983) which were carried aboard the Space Shuttle.

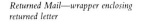

Returned Mail—wrapper enclosing returned letter

Reversed Print (Syria, part of imprint reversed; Peru)

Rocket Mail (Austria, Scottish Western Isles, 1934)

ROMAN TYPE. Fount of type used by printers and distinguishable by its seriffed capitals (i.e. having short cross-lines at the end of the strokes). Roman type was used for the vast majority of postmarks in the British Isles till about 1844, when sans-serif block type was adopted. It is the type-face most commonly used in **overprints** and **surcharges**.

Roman Type

ROTARY CANCELLATION. A device to speed up the cancellation of stamps, the obliterating dies being mounted on a revolving drum, often incorporating a self-inking mechanism. Rotary obliterators were used in some British post offices from the 1850s onwards, but later they were confined mainly to parcels and registered packets. Rotary cancellations, sometimes referred to as revolving stamps or rollers, have also been used in many other countries in recent years and may be recognised by their continuous or repeated impressions.

Rotary Cancellation

ROTARY PERFORATION. A method of perforation which involved the use of toothed perforating wheels operating on the same principle as the normal line perforation, i.e. in one direction across the sheet of stamps, then crosswise.

Rotary Perforation

ROTOGRAVURE. An alternative name for **Photogravure**.

ROUGH PERFORATION. The antithesis of **clean-cut perforation** – showing as holes or teeth with rough edges, imperfectly cut or punched, possibly with circular discs of paper still adhering. This often arises in cases where the perforating pins have become blunt through excessive usage.

Rough Perforation

ROULETTE. French word meaning literally a toothed disc or wheel, used to denote a form of separation in which the paper is merely pierced or cut, but no discs of paper are punched out, as in **perforation**. In philately, the various forms of roulette are alternatively known by French terms preceded by the word percé (pierced). Rouletting was originally performed by a rotary hand tool, but nowadays is carried out by a machine. For the various forms of roulette, *see* Arc, Compound, Cross, Diamond, Experimental, Lozenge, Oblique, Pin, Saw tooth, Serpentine, Serrated and Zigzag.

ROYAL REPRINT. A special printing of the British 1d 1854–7, Plate 66, Die II, on paper watermarked inverted large crown, but without perforations and in black instead of the normal red. This reprint was made in 1864, allegedly at the personal request of Queen Victoria who wished to have some stamps to give to her children, in order to show them what the original Penny Blacks had looked like.

RULED PAPER. Paper ruled with lines as a guide for writing. Such paper was used for stamps of Mexico (1887) and Latvia (1919). ■

St Andrew's Cross (GB Edward VII booklet pane)

SAFETY PAPER. Paper which has been specially treated in the course of manufacture to prevent forgery or illicit cleaning, e.g. the removal of the cancellation. Apart from the **blued** and **chalk-surfaced papers** used for British stamps, one may cite Russian stamps with intersecting chalk lines on their face, the chalk preventing the printing ink from penetrating the paper and making it impossible to remove the postmark without also removing part of the design. Austria used **varnished lines** for the same purpose. Some early stamps of Prussia had an invisible **burélage** which became apparent when attempts were made to clean the stamps. ■

ST ANDREW'S CROSS. A saltire, or cross in which the lines intersect diagonally. This device was printed on the four vacant spaces left in panes of certain early Austrian stamps to prevent the paper being used by forgers. The same device was used on British halfpenny booklet panes (1906–11). The name is also applied to a variant of Edinburgh **double stamp** in which diagonal lines were cut across the obliterating pillar.

SAMPLE LABELS AND STAMPS. Labels and imitations of stamps produced by firms of security printers to show to prospective clients the capabilities of different printing processes. Waterlow and Sons, for example, printed small sheets of actual stamp designs, in different colours, overprinted to denote their status, or punched with holes. Many printers since the mid-19th century have produced labels inscribed SAMPLE or its equivalent in other languages, and these are sometimes given away at demonstrations in trade shows and philatelic exhibitions.

Sample Labels—De La Rue & Co.

SANS-SERIF TYPE. A fount of type used by printers, distinguished by the lack of cross-lines at the end of the strokes. This style is also known as block lettering, and has been used by the British Post Office for most datestamps since 1845. It is also a popular fount used in overprints and surcharges. *See also* Roman and Seriffed type.

Sans-Serif Type

SAW-TOOTH ROULETTE. Alternatively known by its French name *Percé en scie* and characterised by large cuts made in a zigzag pattern.

Saw-Tooth Roulette—La Guaira (Venezuela) local 'packet' post

SCIENTIFIC EXPEDITIONS. Stamps have been overprinted or specially printed for the use of expeditions of science and exploration. They were officially sanctioned by New Zealand for Shackleton's expedition to King Edward VII Land (1908) and Scott's Expedition to Victoria Land (1911). British stamps were to have been overprinted for use at Tristan da Cunha, Enderby Land and Gough Island by the Shackleton-Rowett Expedition of 1922, but the issue was aborted following Shackleton's death. Unofficial stamps have also been produced in connexion with many expeditions, ranging from Dr Bruce's Scotia Antarctic Expedition (1904) to the Dahlak Archipelago Expedition (1969). In the same genre may be considered the blue label for the 1924 Mount Everest Expedition.

Scientific Expeditions (Antarctica)

SCOTS LOCAL CANCELLATIONS. Cancellations in the form of the undated name stamps used at minor post offices in Scotland. Some offices were permitted to cancel outgoing mail as an experiment authorised in 1854, but it was later extended to all sub offices in Scotland and continued until early 1860 when undated stamps were withdrawn from all minor offices in the UK. These cancellations are much sought after, on account of their unusual appearance and the variety of colours used during the six year period of currency. The term "Scots Locals" is also applied loosely to the postmarks of these undated stamps found on the backs of covers. Their use as backstamps covered a much longer period, from the early 1840s till 1860.

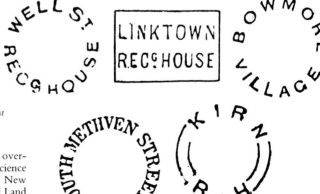

Scots Local Cancellations

SCOUT POSTS. Postal services operated by Boy Scouts, usually in times of emergency. The first of these was that organised by Colonel Baden-Powell during the siege of Mafeking (1900); Cadet Sergeant Major Warner Goodyear, portrayed on the 3d stamp, has been described as the first Scout on a stamp. Baden-Powell, fonder of the Scout movement, was portrayed on the 1d stamp. The Scouts in Prague organised the first postal service of Czechoslovakia (1918), while Scouts operated the guerrilla postal service during the Warsaw Rising (1944). *See also* Christmas charity post stamps.

Seals

Scout Posts—Baden Powell's Mafeking post (1900)

SCRIPT TYPE. A printer's type approximating to handwriting, and used in many watermarks, as well as some overprints.

SEALING LABELS. Gummed or self-adhesive labels, produced singly, in sheets or coils, used by postal authorities to reseal broken packets or those which have been opened for censorship, Customs examination or to ascertain the sender for return in cases of non-delivery.

Sealing Label (used at Penrith PO, 1905)

SEALS. Gummed labels intended to seal envelopes and wrappers by affixing them across the ends or flaps. Seals of this type include Egyptian **interpostals** and the scalloped wafers used by many German government departments on official mail. The term is also applied loosely to charity labels, e.g. **Christmas** and **Easter** seals.

SECRET MARKS. Minuscule marks in stamp designs, made by the designers, engravers or printers to identify their work. Examples are Cuba's 10c of 1889 and 1905–7, the latter having a small white ball added to the extension of the name panel by the American Bank Note Company to distinguish its work. The US 1c of 1870 and 1873 (Benjamin Franklin) are similarly distinguished, the latter having a small line on the pearl to the left of the figure 1 to identify the Continental Bank Note Company. Stamps of Jersey issued during the German occupation had tiny A's in the corners, which the designer, Major Rybot, later explained as signifying *Ad Avernum, Adolfe Atrox* ("To Hell with you, awful Adolf"). Since 1935 most Canadian stamps have had the date worked into the design in microscopic numerals, while British letterpress stamps produced by Somerset House and De La Rue used **date cuts** in the marginal rule to identify different printings.

Secret Mark (Cuba—ball added)

Security Overprint—Greek characters added to deter forgery

SECURITY OVERPRINT. A device used by Macao for definitive stamps overprinted in 1934 for airmail. Greek characters were included to render forgery more difficult.

SEEBECK ISSUES. Stamps produced by the Hamilton Bank Note Company of New York for Ecuador (1892–6), Honduras (1890–5), Nicaragua (1890–9) and El Salvador (1890–9), the designs being changed annually. Their nickname is derived from Nicholas F. Seebeck, an American entrepreneur who negotiated deals with the governments of these Latin American companies whereby he undertook to supply them with new issues each year free of charge, on condition that he could retain the printing plates and unsold remainders. Seebeck used the plates to reprint stamps which were then dumped on the philatelic market.

SELF-SERVICE REGISTRATION STAMPS. Stamps combining the features of **registration labels** with the fee for special handling, issued by the German Democratic Republic in 1967–8 for letter packets and parcels. These stamps were issued in pairs from automatic vending machines, together with a certificate of posting, against a 50pf coin. One label was affixed to the letter and the other retained by the sender affixed to the certificate of posting. These stamps closely resembled the registration labels then in use, but had the value inscribed at the top, and "Gebuhr bezahlt" (postage paid) at the foot. They also incorporated the abbreviation "SbPA" – *Selbstbedienungs Postamt* (self-service post office).

SELVAGE (SELVEDGE). The marginal paper surrounding a sheet of stamps or labels, popularly known as "stamp edging".

Seebeck Issues

Selvage (GB definitive with margin)

SELF-ADHESIVE LABELS AND STAMPS. Labels and stamps with a rubber-based adhesive that does not require to be moistened. Stamps of this type were pioneered by Sierra Leone in 1964 and since then issued by Montserrat, Norfolk Island and Tonga among others. These stamps have to be peeled off backing paper which is often used as an **advertising** medium. The same principle has been applied to registration, airmail and other kinds of postal labels in many countries since the late 1970s.

SEMI-OFFICIAL STAMPS. Stamps used in connexion with private postal services, but having official sanction. In this category come many airmail stamps of Canada and Colombia, the **railway letter fee stamps** of the UK, and the **zemstvo** issues of Russia. *See also* Local stamps.

Self-adhesive stamp (Sierra Leone 1964)

Semi-Official Stamps (Brazil 'Condor', Canada 'Laurentide Air Service, Colombia 'SCADTA')

SEMI-POSTALS. American term for stamps bearing a premium in excess of regular postage, i.e. **charity stamps**.

SENSITISED PAPER. Paper treated with a light-sensitive ferro-prussiate compound for reproducing draughtsman's drawings, but used for the siege stamps of Mafeking in 1900.

SERIAL NUMBERING. A means of controlling and checking the issue of stamps, which are often thus numbered in the sheet margin. Some issues of Spain, Andorra and Spanish colonies had serial numbers on the reverse of each stamp. Serial numbering is also a feature of labels intended for registration, certified, insured or recorded delivery mail, international or receipted parcels, Royal Mail Special Delivery and other special services. Some of the companies issuing **railway letter fee** stamps overprinted serial numbers on each stamp.

SERIFFED TYPE. A fount of printer's type distinguished by serifs or cross-lines on the ends of the strokes. *See also* Roman type.

SERPENTINE ROULETTE. Otherwise known by the French term *Percé en serpentine*, a form of separation in which the cuts are in a wavy line pattern, interrupted in the centre of each "wave" to prevent the sheets from falling apart. When the stamps are separated the uncut portion appears in the form of a small "shoulder".

Serpentine Roulette (Finnish stamp and local post issues)

Serial Numbering—sheet number in margin

SERRATED ROULETTE. A roulette characterised by small, semi-circular cuts. It is, in fact, a very fine-gauge variant of the **arc roulette**.

Serrated Roulette (Tasmania)

Se-tenant (Rumania and Brazil different designs; Belgium, one stamp surcharged; Gabon narrow and wide settings)

SE-TENANT. French expression signifying "joined together", used to describe adjoining stamps or labels which differ from each other in value, inscription, design, colour or some other respect, such as one overprinted or surcharged, and the other not. Stamp **booklets** and **coil strips** often include different stamps side by side, but this practice has become increasingly fashionable in sheets of stamps where it is used to create **composite** designs.

SET-OFF. A form of **reversed print**, caused by laying a sheet of stamps on another printed sheet which has been insufficiently dried, resulting in a transfer of the design images to the gummed underside of the upper sheet, in reverse. A similar variety can occur in printing if a sheet of paper fails to be taken up by the rollers, and a "wild" impression on the underlay or impression cylinder is transferred to the back of the next sheet, known as a "blanket print". ∎

SETTING. Type for printing is composed or set by the compositor, hence a setting is a particular arrangement or grouping of movable types or **cliches** forming a plate or single unit. The term is used principally in connexion with over-printed and/or surcharged stamps where there may be one setting, i.e. plate, for a sheet of stamps, or perhaps four or six matrices or stereotyped plates to make up the sheet. In the latter event the actual formation of the whole plate may be deduced by the study of individual cliches – distinctive flaws such as broken letters or other irregularities would be recurring at fixed intervals on the plate. In the same way, second and third settings, etc. may be identified.

Settings (Rhodesia 'Half Penny' and 'Half-Penny', Turks & Caicos Is.—different settings of WAR TAX)

SETTING ERROR. A cliche laid down sideways or upside down in relation to the others on a printing plate or lithographic stone. *See also* Tête-bêche.

Setting Error—one stamp turned sideways!

SHADE. A variety or degree of colour – in philately the term implies a variation, gradation or difference in the tonal depth. A shade ceases to be such when the variation is sufficiently marked to alter the basic colour of the stamp. For example, a green stamp tending towards blue-green and turquoise would, if the progression continued, become greenish blue, i.e. basically blue. Shades usually occur in new printings of definitive stamps when the printers are unable to match exactly the printing inks used in the original or preceding issue, or when climatic changes take place. Marked shades, which may be linked to specific printings of stamps and the relative sheet cylinder or plate numbers, are recorded in the Gibbons catalogues (except *Stamps of the World*), but not where there is a whole range of intermediate shades. ■

SHEET. Stamps are printed on sheets of paper trimmed to convenient size, or, if printed "on the web" (i.e. on continuous reels) subsequently guillotined to "sheet" size. The size of a sheet and the number of stamps contained within it may vary from the very small (e.g. Ethiopia and Czechoslovakia, 4 stamps in normal sheet form) to the British halfpenny stamps of 1870–9 which were in sheets of 480. Most British low values till 1971 were issued in sheets of 240, while high values were in sheets of 40 or even 20. Since 1971 low values have been in sheets of 200 and other countries with a decimal currency system have used 50 or 100 subjects per sheet. Some of the smaller Commonwealth countries in recent years have issued stamps in sheets of 20 or 30 subjects, for operational economic reasons. Modern Swedish stamps are not issued in sheets at all, but either in rolls for automatic vending machines, or in booklets. *See also* Imprint, Margin, Marginal Guide Marks, Marginal Inscriptions, Miniature Sheet and Selvage.

SHEET NUMBER. *See* Serial Numbering.

SHEET WATERMARK. Alternative term for an All-over watermark.

Sheet (GB 1967 Christmas stamp with Queen's head missing error) (opposite)

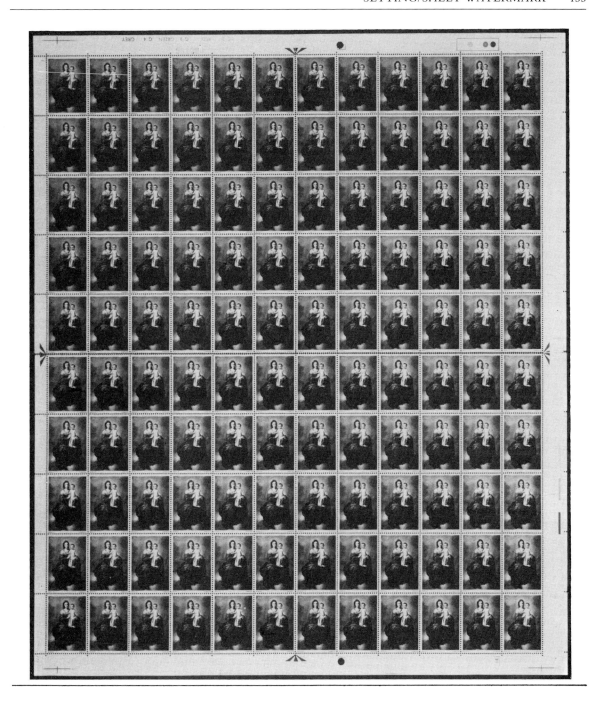

Sheetlet (New Zealand Health stamps)

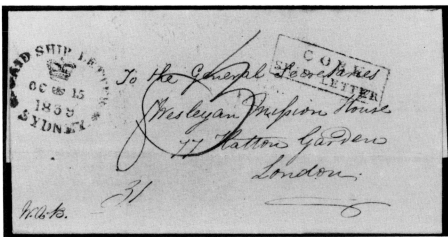

Ship Letter (Cork, Ireland, 1839)

SHEETLET. A sheet of stamps containing a much smaller number of subjects than the normal sheet format. Although stamps are known to have been issued in sheets containing as few as four stamps since 1894 (Ethiopia), the term is applied mainly to some modern issues (e.g. New Zealand Health stamps) issued in small sheets for the convenience of customers, as well as in sheets of 100 for post office counter use. Many countries (e.g. Liechtenstein, Cook Islands) issue commemorative stamps in small sheets, sometimes including a label or coupon to make up the format. Sheetlets are also sometimes issued in different colours, or with different perforations, from normal sheet stamps. *See also* Miniature Sheet.

SHIP LETTER. A letter conveyed by private vessel, as distinct from a **packet letter**. The carriage of ship letters was first regulated by an Act of 1660, and from the 1760s until the beginning of the 20th century many British seaports marked such letters with distinctive postmarks. Up to 1840 the need to distinguish ship letters from packet letters and inland mail was governed by the special rates of postage applicable. India letters were a particular type of ship letter brought to Britain by ships of the East India Company which were subject to a special arrangement. India letter postmarks went out of use in the 1840s, as mail contracts were awarded to the steamship companies. Other countries also had ship letter regulations, and marked such mail with the equivalent in other languages. The use of ship letter marks died out after the Universal Postal Union adopted the **paquebot** classification in 1894.

SHIPPING COMPANY STAMPS. Stamps issued by shipping firms to prepay postage on mail conveyed by their vessels. The earliest of these was the Lady McLeod 5c produced in 1847 by David Bryce of Trinidad. Subsequent issues were made by the Pacific Steam Navigation Co. (1858–9), Gauthier Freres (1856–7), the Turkish Admiralty (1859), St Thomas and La Guaira (1864–9), ROPiT (1865–1914), the Danubian Steamship Co (1866–74), TB Morton (1866–72), St Lucia Steam Conveyance Co (1870–2) and Hamburg-American (HAPAG) Line (1876), among others.

SHRINKAGE. Contraction of paper resulting from dampening and then drying, as part of the **intaglio** process. Uneven shrinkage of the paper caused problems for the perforator, resulting in badly centred stamps. Shrinkage also caused minute variations in the actual size of stamps or their design images, exemplified by stamps of Chile (Columbus issue, 1905–9) and Gibraltar (KGV issue, 1931–3).

SIDEWAYS WATERMARK. Watermark sideways in relation to the stamp image, usually arising from the format of the stamp making it more convenient to print them sideways on. The special arrangements for printing British coil stamps for use in firms' automatic dispensing machines with left side delivery resulted in sideways watermarks, and this was also a feature of stamps from certain small stamp **booklets**.

SIEGE POSTMARKS AND STAMPS. The transmission of mail from towns under siege has produced a wide range of distinctive markings, and even special postal stationery and stamps. Examples of special markings and stationery may be cited from the sieges of Venice (1848), Metz (1870), Paris (1870–1), Adrianople (1913), Przemysl (1915), and Warsaw (1944) while stamps specially printed or overprinted in connexion with siege posts include those used at Mafeking and Schweizer Renecke (both 1900). *See also* Balloon Posts, Submarine Mail.

Sideways Watermark (Dominica, 1921 1d., sideways Mult. Script CA watermark)

Siege Postmark—cover despatched by balloon from Siege of Paris (1870)

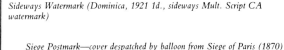

Shipping Company Stamp (Royal Mail Steam Packet Company)

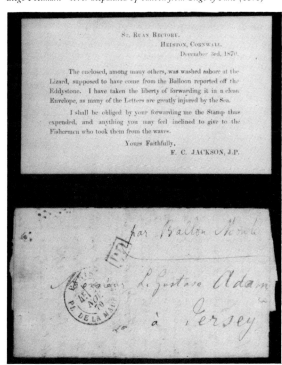

Siege stamp— Mafeking, 1900

SILK THREAD PAPER. A form of safety paper with coloured silk threads embedded in it. Paper of this type was devised by John **Dickinson** and used for British embossed adhesives and postal stationery. It was also used for stamps of Bavaria (1849–68) and Switzerland (1854–62). ∎

SIMULATED PERFORATION. *See* Imitation Perforation.

SINGLE WATERMARK. A watermark device arranged so that each stamp bears a single impression.

Single Watermark—Single Crown CA, Springbok's Head

SINKING FUND STAMPS. Stamps overprinted or inscribed "Caisse d'Amortissement" or CA, issued by France (1927–31) for postage but carrying a premium in aid of a fund for the reduction of the national debt.

Single Watermark

Sinking Fund Stamps

SKELETON HANDSTAMP. A datestamp with slots around its circumference for the insertion of loose type, to make up the name of a post office, either a temporary office at an exhibition or special event, or one whose normal datestamp has been lost, stolen, damaged or destroyed. Such stamps, known variously as skeletons, temporary stamps, travellers or relief cancellers, were adopted by the British Post Office in 1839 and are used to this day, mainly in emergencies. They are also used extensively in other Commonwealth countries, notably Guyana, Nigeria and New Zealand, and also in the Irish Republic. Apart from the unevenness of their lettering they are usually characterised by their diameter which is often much larger than normal. Irish skeletons often had a double rim, while some Scottish skeletons had a dotted rim.

Skeleton Handstamps (GB, New Zealand)

SLOGAN POSTMARK. A postmark bearing some form of announcement or message, advertisement or propaganda. Handstamps were used in 1661–75 to advertise the Kent and Essex posts, but the idea was not revived until 1893 when a slogan die was incorporated in American cancelling machines to publicise the Columbian Exposition in Chicago. Thereafter slogans were used to publicise exhibitions and fairs in Canada (1901), the USA (1904), Belgium (1910) and New Zealand (1912), and the Oberammergau Passion Play in Bavaria (1910).

Machine slogans were first used by Britain in 1917 to publicise war bonds. After the First World War, slogans were extended to postal or government announcements. Local publicity slogans appeared in France and the USA in 1921 and spread to other countries in the late 1920s, but were not adopted by Britain till 1963. Slogans are normally placed to the right of the dater die, but in the 1960s and 1970s many British slogans were "transposed", i.e. placed on the left, so that they would be clear of the postage stamps. Many postage meters since 1922 have had firms' slogans fitted.

Slogan Postmarks—hand and machine applied

SLURRED PRINT. Otherwise known as a Smudged print, this is an indistinct blur or doubling of an image caused by "paper slip" at the point of contact with the printing cylinder or plate, and not a **double print** in the true sense. This defect is sometimes caused by insufficient wiping of excess ink off the plate prior to printing. ∎

SOLDIERS' STAMPS. Stamps issued by many countries to denote the exemption of servicemen's mail from postage, or special concessionary rates applicable in such cases. Such stamps include the unofficial Army Franks (USA) and the Melilla labels (Spain), but the most prolific of these issues are those which have been produced by Switzerland for every regiment, squadron and unit since the First World War period. *See also* Franchise Stamps, Free Mail, Guerrilla Stamps and Military Posts.

SOUVENIR CARD. A large-sized card produced by the US Bureau of Engraving and Printing on behalf of the USPO and intended as a memento of international philatelic exhibitions. These cards have been issued since the Philympia Exhibition in London (1970) and were originally intended to be given away as souvenirs of visits to the USPO stand at such exhibitions. As a rule they bear enlarged reproductions of obsolete American stamps which are linked in some way to the country hosting the exhibition, and have a descriptive text printed below.

Soldiers' Stamp

Souvenir Card—issued by US Post Office for international stamp exhibition

Spandrel (Monaco, GB)

Souvenir Sheet (Sharjah)

SOUVENIR SHEET. Term which is sometimes used loosely as a synonym for a **miniature sheet** but which ought more properly be confined to (a) small sheets which have postal validity but do not incorporate a stamp or stamps of conventional form; and (b) small sheets of philatelic interest but no postal validity. In the first category come sheets which are, in fact, very large stamps, issued singly without perforations, with an over-all decorative motif. In the second category come the gummed souvenirs of STAMPEX and other philatelic exhibitions, often reproducing stamps, but not possessing any postal validity.

SPANDREL. The space between the exterior curves of an arch and an enclosing right angle. In stamps it may be regarded as the space beteen the outer rectangular border or frame and the central circle or oval enclosing the main part of the design.

SPECIAL DELIVERY LABELS AND STAMPS. Labels denoting special handling and stamps prepaying the handling fees, in connexion with various services akin to **express** mail. The terms are often synonymous, although strictly speaking "express" means accelerated transmission of mail, whereas special delivery implies the acceleration of mail only from the delivery office to the addressee. The United States pioneered stamps for this purpose, in 1885. At first they could only be used for immediate delivery at Special Delivery offices, but three years later this facility was extended to all delivery offices. Other countries issuing such stamps include Canada, New Zealand, Italy and Mexico. Both Canada and the USA have also issued special delivery airmail stamps.

Spandrel (India, Nevis)

Special Delivery Stamp (Canada)

SPECIAL EVENT POSTMARK. A postmark, usually handstruck but occasionally applied by machine, used at or in connexion with a special event of a temporary nature. These have been used at temporary exhibition post offices since 1855 but in more recent years many of these, particularly the pictorial types, are applied to mail posted in special posting-boxes or sent under cover to postmasters at permanent offices temporarily equipped with such handstamps. The postal administrations of the UK and the crown dependencies (Isle of Man and the Channel Islands) make a charge for such philatelic mail, but other countries operate a return posting facility at no additional cost.

SPECIAL FEE STAMPS. Stamps denoting the fees payable in respect of special handling of mail. Such facilities include **Late Fee**, **Certified Mail**, **Marine Insurance**, **Personal Delivery** and **Registration**. Danish stamps overprinted or inscribed "Gebyr" or "Gebyrmaerke" were used to indicate the payment of special handling fees, including the late registration of letters. The USPO uses labels inscribed "Fragile" on delicate packets, but incorporates an inscription signifying that a fee has been paid to secure greater care in transit.

SPECIAL FLIGHT STAMPS. Stamps issued by the Netherlands and Switzerland for use on mail carried on special flights. The Dutch stamps were inscribed "Bijzondere Vluchten" whereas the Swiss stamps were inscribed **"Pro Aero"**.

Special Event Postmark—Liverpool International Garden Festival, 1984

Special Flight Stamps (Newfoundland)

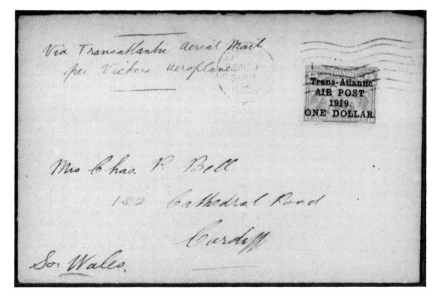

SPECIMEN STAMPS. Samples of new stamps, distributed to the various postal administrations of the world through the headquarters of the Universal Postal Union, for purposes of identification and record. These stamps are distinguished by the overprint "Specimen", or its equivalent in other languages, e.g. "Muestra" (Spanish), "Monster" (Dutch), "Muester" (German) or "Obrasetz" (Russian), as a security measure to prevent postal use. Stamps thus overprinted are also sometimes distributed for publicity purposes.

Specimen Stamps

Split Stamps

SPLIT STAMPS. Stamps which have been divided up for use as temporary denominations whose value is proportionate to the size of the fraction. The commonest type is a **bisect**, but stamps have been known divided into thirds, **quarters** or eighths. *See also* Fractional Stamps.

SPONSORED BOOKLETS, STAMPS AND POST-MARKS. The underwriting of the costs of production and/or distribution by some body other than the postal authority making the issue. Many **special event** and **slogan postmarks** are sponsored either by government departments, tourist and civic authorities, commercial firms and charitable institutions who often publish souvenir covers and cards in association with these postmarks. Sponsored booklets arose out of the practice of selling advertising space in the interleaving and covers. In 1959 the British Post Office produced a 2s booklet sponsored by the Bacon Council and this was followed by similar booklets sponsored by insurance companies, a feature being that all the advertising in these booklets was confined to the sponsors. Sponsorship of stamp issues has been more covert, but it explains some of the more obviously commercial subject matter of some recent commemoratives.

Sponsored Booklet (Stanley Gibbons, 1982) and Postmarks (GB slogans)

SPOON CANCELLATIONS. Experimental duplex cancellations of England and Wales which derive their nickname from the fact that the integral dater portion is oval, like the bowl of a spoon. These postmarks were in use between 1853 and 1860 and many of them are of considerable rarity.

SQUARED CIRCLES. The first type of combined **date** and **obliterating stamps** used in England and Wales, and current between 1879 and the First World War, although isolated examples are recorded till the 1930s. These postmarks derive their name from the rectangular corners and concentric arcs surrounding the central date circle. Squared circles were also used by Canada and Italy at the turn of the century.

Spoon Cancellation

Squared Circle cancels (London, Market Rasen)

STAMP. A device or instrument for stamping, hence also the impression or mark made by stamping or printing, a printed or stamped piece of paper that for some restricted purpose is used as a token of credit (e.g. a postage stamp), or occasionally of debit (e.g. a postage due label). When Rowland Hill spoke of stamps in 1838–9 he had in mind a handstruck or printed impression indicating the prepayment of postage, mainly a stamped letter sheet or wrapper; and only considered "small pieces of gummed paper bearing the stamp" as an after-thought. Postage stamps may be handstruck (e.g. the **Dockwra** stamps of 1680–2), impressed on postal stationery, or printed on gummed labels to be affixed to postal packets. Collectors restrict the use of "stamp" to labels prepaying postage, as opposed to seals, stickers and other pieces of gummed paper without postal validity.

Stamp Duty

Stamp—British Guiana 1856 1c.—the World's rarest stamp

STAMP CURRENCY. *See* Encased Postage Stamps, Fractional Currency and Postage Currency.

STAMP DUTY. An inscription commonly found on **fiscal stamps**, but also found on the early postage stamps of the Australian states and New Zealand. These are classified as **Postal Fiscals**, with the exception of the stamps issued by Victoria from 1884. The Victoria Government's Postage Act of 1883 decreed that stamps of the three existing types – postage, duty and fee – should henceforward be interchangeable, and that there should be only one multi-purpose series in use from the beginning of 1885. These continued to be inscribed STAMP DUTY up to and including the issues of 1896–9.

STAMPED PAPER. Paper bearing an impressed or embossed **fiscal stamp** intended for a non-postal purpose. ∎

STAMPLESS COVER. A cover, wrapper or letter-sheet which has passed through the post since the advent of adhesive stamps in the country of origin, but which does not bear either adhesive or imprinted stamps. In this category come covers bearing handstruck or machine-applied Paid or Official Paid marks, even though these are, strictly speaking, postage stamps of a sort. The term is at its most precise when describing **free mail**, forces' mail on active service, or covers which have been endorsed in some way to indicate that stamps were unavailable, either in wartime or in times of financial upheaval (e.g. the German hyper-inflation of 1923). Similarly **metered** and **permit mail** and items bearing **postage paid impressions** cannot be regarded as stampless in any real sense.

STEREOTYPE. A solid metallic plate for printing, cast from a plastic mould of movable types. The Cape of Good Hope "Woodblocks" were engraved on steel and printed from stereotyped plates.

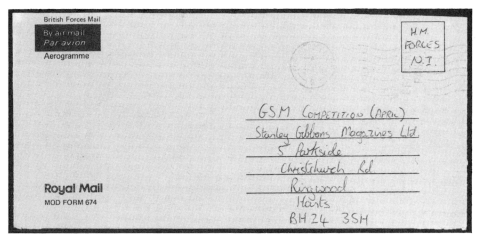

Stampless Cover—Forces mail from Northern Ireland

Stitch Watermark (USA 3c. of 1870)

Straight Edge

Stereotype—the rare Cape of Good Hope 'Woodblock'

STITCH WATERMARK. Extraneous portions of a normal watermark, caused by stitches in the web - cloth or wire - on which the paper is manufactured. Good examples of this may be found on US stamps.

STRAIGHT EDGE. The imperforate side(s) of a normally-perforated stamp, commonly found among American and Canadian stamps, due to the division of **gutter** margins between sheets or panes by guillotine. Stamps from booklets and coils or rolls are also found with straight edges which, however, are generally termed "imperforate at side", and may be deliberate or accidental. *See also* Trimmed.

STRIKE POSTS. Emergency postal services operated by local authorities or even private individuals during postal strikes. The first of these was run by Arthur Banta between San Francisco and Fresno (1894). Subsequent services include strike posts at Amiens (1909), Milan (1920), Linz-Vienna (1924), Orleans-Loiret (1953), British Columbia (1965, 1968), Albany, NY (1970) and Dublin (1980). Both France (1968) and Britain (1962, 1964 and 1971) have had nationwide go-slows or strikes which resulted in numerous local services. In the 1971 strike alone about 500 different services operated, and special stamps were not only issued by these services, but the Cook Islands overprinted stamps in connexion with one of these services which handled overseas mail.

STRIP. Three or more stamps joined in a single row, horizontal or vertical.

SUBMARINE MAIL. Postal services operated by submarines in time of war when normal means of seaborne communication are disrupted. The first service operated between Germany and the USA in 1916–17 and special stamps from 5 to 100 marks were issued for this purpose. In 1938, during the Spanish Civil War, communications between the Balearic Islands and the mainland were maintained by submarines and six stamps and a miniature sheet were issued in this connexion. During the Second World War three submarine posts had their own stamps: the Italian Base Atlantica at Bordeaux (1943), the

Strip (se-tenant, three different designs)

Strike Posts (Cook Is. surcharge, private issues during 1971 British Postal Strike)

Submarine Mail (USA, 1970)

German service to and from Crete, Vukovar, Rhodes and Leros (1944–5) and the beleaguered garrison at Hela, Danzig (March–May 1945). Souvenir covers, with special cachets and handstamps, are known from the Royal Navy and US Navy (e.g. the Clyde Submarine Base, Helensburgh and the Polaris Base, Holy Loch.)

SULPHURETTED. Sometimes, though incorrectly, described as "oxidised", it pertains to certain stamps in shades or red, yellow or orange which have turned deep brown or black due to atmospheric pollution reacting chemically with pigments such as vermilion (mercuric sulphide) in the printing ink. ■

SUNDAY DELIVERY STAMPS. Special stamps incorporating an additional fee were issued by Bulgaria in 1925–9 and 1942 for mail intended to be delivered on Sundays and public holidays. The revenue from the additional fees was used to maintain a sanatorium and rest homes for postal employees and their families. *See also* Dominical Labels.

Sunday Delivery Stamp (Bulgaria)

Superimposed Adhesive Stamp (North German Federation, 1868)

SUPERIMPOSED ADHESIVE STAMPS. Ordinary postage stamps affixed over imprinted stamps on postal stationery by the North German Confederation in 1868 for various member states. A security overprint was applied in order to tie the adhesive to the cover before issue to the public. In recent

years adhesive **postage paid impressions** have often been used to convert firms' stationery bearing a previous PPI to a new class or postage.

SURCHARGE. An **overprint** which alters or emphasises a stamp's face value. Most surcharges come into the first category, but the only examples from Britain were the 3d and 6d lilac of 1883, with the values overprinted in red ink to make them more prominent. Generally speaking, however, surcharges are made during temporary shortages of certain denominations. Normally the surcharge is **typeset**, but manuscript surcharge was used in Trinidad (1882) and typewritten surcharges were applied at Tonga (1896), Battambang, Thailand (1902) and at Long Island, Smyrna (1916) to convert Turkish fiscals to postal use by British occupying forces. The term Surcharge is also used to denote the additional sum due from the recipients of unpaid or underpaid mail to cover the deficiency, fine and/or handling charges where applicable.

Surcharge

SURFACE PRINTING. *See* Letterpress.

SUSSE PERFORATION. A coarse perforation gauging 7, unofficially applied by Susse Freres of Paris in 1861 to French imperforate stamps, as a convenience for their customers.

SYLLABIC ALPHABETS. Two alphabets, known as Kata Kana and Hira Kana, used in Japan for the transliteration of foreign names and loan-words which cannot conveniently be written in Kanji script. Some 23 of the Kata Kana letters were utilised in marking the 1874 series of Japanese stamps to distinguish them from the 1872– 3 series and may thus be classified as **secret marks**.

Syllabic Alphabet (Japan, 1874)

TAB. An appendage to a stamp in the form of an attached coupon . The **Dominical labels** used by Belgium were a form of tab, but the term is usually confined to the stamps of Israel which, since 1948, have had pictorial and/or descriptive motifs relating to the stamp designs. One may also include certain issues of France, New Zealand and South Africa (mainly booklets) with **advertisements** on the sheet or pane margins.

Tab attached to Israeli stamp

TAGGED STAMPS. Stamps overprinted with **phosphor** bands to assist the electronic sorting of mail. The term is mainly used in Canada and the United States.

Tagged Stamps (Canada)

TAILLE DOUCE. French term for **Intaglio**.

TALKING STAMPS. An issue of seven stamps by Bhutan in 1973, in the form of miniature gramophone records which played the national anthem and provided a commentary on the history of the country. The stamps were made of plastic with a self-adhesive backing.

Talking Stamp (Bhutan, 1973)

TAXE. French word for "tax" or "charge", used by member countries of the Universal Postal Union to denote foreign unpaid or underpaid mail. Marks thus inscribed, or with a prominent T, alert the office of exchange or the delivery office in the country of destination that a **surcharge** should be levied on the addressee. The word also appears in **postage due labels** in the phrase "Taxe a Percevoir" (Tax to collect), and in **handstruck postage stamps** as "Taxe Percue" (Charge paid).

Taxe (France, Postage Due)

TAXPOST. A service of the British Post Office, introduced in 1984 as a variant of **Datapost** to expedite the correspondence of Inland Revenue offices. Distinctive red and yellow labels thus inscribed are employed in this connexion.

Taxpost—British Post Office label

TELEGRAPH STAMPS, STATIONERY AND CANCELLATIONS. Adhesive or impressed stamps intended solely for the prepayment of telegraphic communications are usually attached to or printed on the message form, although in some cases they may be affixed to a document which is then cut in half, one portion being retained by the telegraph office and the other handed to the sender as a receipt. Distinctive stamps were issued by the private telegraph companies in Britain and Ireland between 1851 and 1869, and after the service was nationalised special stamps were issued by the Post Office from 1876 to 1881. Telegraph stamps have also been issued by many other countries down to the present time. In many cases, however, postage stamps are used telegraphically, and may often be differentiated by the form of cancellation used. In the UK, for example, railway stations and non-postal agencies empowered to transmit telegrams used framed numerical cancellations from 1870 to 1893 when undated oval brass stamps were supplied. The latter continued to be employed till 1935. A wide variety of special stationery has also been produced in connexion with the telegraph services, ranging from the message forms completed by the sender, and the telegrams delivered to the recipient, to the distinctive forms used for radiotelegrams, ship to shore telegrams and greetings telegrams. Other variants include priority labels, overnight and weekend registered telegrams, and confirmation telegrams. *See also* Military Telegraphs.

Telegraph stamps

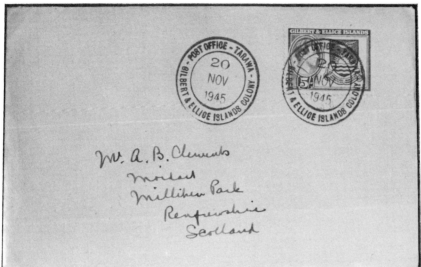

Temporary Rubber Datestamp (Gilbert & Ellice Is.)

Testing Labels—GB blank and inscribed 'Poached Eggs'

Tête-Bêche

TEMPORARY RUBBER DATESTAMP. Sometimes abbreviated to TRD, it denotes a form of cancellation used in some West Indian and Pacific island groups. Theoretically, as the name implies, these datestamps are used in emergency, but there are many instances of them being used over a period of years. Like the **Climax** daters of the British Isles, it is more probable that they were intended for permanent use, but were confined to offices of minor importance which did not merit the expense of a steel datestamp.

TESTING LABELS. Stamp-sized gummed labels, in coils or booklets, used by postal administrations to test the efficient working of automatic vending machines. These labels have no postal validity but occasionally examples, such as the famous Poached Egg label , have been affixed to mail and gone through the post undetected.

TÊTE-BÊCHE. A French idiom (literally "head-spade") with the philatelic meaning of a pair of stamps in which one is upside-down in relation to the other. This arrangement sometimes occurred accidentally, as a result of a **cliche** being inserted in a forme upside down. In modern times, however, it occurs in the printing of sheets of stamps in small panes for booklets, adjoining panes being upside down in relation to each other to facilitate separation. Occasionally uncut panes come on to the market and stamps from neighbouring rows form *tête-bêche* pairs.

TEXTILES AS PRINTING MATERIALS. Stamps printed on cloth were first issued by Hungary in September 1958, waxed cloth being used for a miniature sheet of four stamps honouring the International Philatelic Congress in Brussels. Silk rayon was used by Bhutan for a set of 1969 depicting prayer banners. ∎

THEMATIC COLLECTING. Otherwise known as "thematics" or "topical collecting", this is a popular method of collecting stamps with a specific pictorial subject or theme, such as Birds, Flowers, Ships, Sport and many others. Virtually every modern stamp can be related to one or more themes. Nowadays thematic collectors extend their interest to postal stationery and pictorial postmarks related to their chosen theme.

THERMOGRAPHY. Printing process whose name is derived from the Greek meaning "heat writing" and alludes to the production of a pattern in raised relief by heating a resinous compound. It was first used philatelically in 1965 in a set of overprints by Sierra Leone in honour of Sir Winston Churchill. It was combined with **lithography** by Turkey to produce several commemorative issues of 1966–8. The local stamps used by the Moulins, Timaru bicycle post of New Zealand were printed by thermography. ∎

THERMOPLASTICS. An alternative name for **thermography**, but more properly applied to stamps which are actually produced in plastic substances, e.g. Bhutan's issues simulating the bas-relief of sculpture, the rough texture of oil-paintings and the laminated prismatic-ribbed plastic surfaces which provided three-dimensional effects. ∎

TIED. Adhesive stamps "married" to the original envelope, postcard or wrapper, by the cancellation which extends beyond the confines of the stamp on to the postal matter, and thus confirming the genuine use of the original item. The term is also applied to stamps "on piece", and is particularly desirable in the case of **bisected stamps** used in the post.

TIN CAN MAIL. A postal service instituted at Niuafo'ou, Tonga in 1882 as a means of getting canisters of letters through the surf to mail-boats anchored offshore. The service was taken over in 1932 by Walt Quensell who applied up to 23 different colourful Tin Can Mail cachets to outgoing correspondence. Stamps were issued by Tonga and Niuafo'ou in 1982 to commemorate the centenary of the service. The St Kilda Tin Can Mail, practised by the British Army and National Trust since 1958, is a modern and sophisticated variant of the St Kilda "mailboats" – hollowed pieces of wood used by the islanders to transmit messages by ocean current to the Scottish mainland, a method dating from 1734 to the 1930s. Special cachets thus inscribed have been used in recent years.

Tied (Kuwait stamp on piece)

Tin Can Mail (Tonga)

TINTED PAPER. Paper slightly toned on one side, usually to assist the printer to avoid printing stamps on the gummed side. This device was used by Britain for later printings of the 6d embossed stamp, a greenish tint being used on the gummed side, and also by Hanover, which used a reddish tint for the same purpose. ∎

TO PAY LABELS. Labels denoting charges to be recovered from the addressee and thus distinguished from **postage due labels** because the charges related to Customs and special handling fees rather than deficient postage as such. GB labels thus inscribed include the higher denominations (1924–63) and all postage due labels since 1970. The Isle of Man (1973), Jersey (high values of 1969 and all values from 1971) and Guernsey (since 1982) have also issued To Pay labels.

To Pay Label (GB, 1971)

TOO LATE. Inscription on postmarks to explain apparent delay to mail, which had been posted too late to connect with the last despatch of that day. It is also found on some **late fee stamps**.

Too Late postmarks

TOPICAL COLLECTING. American term for **thematic collecting**.

TOUGHRA. A **paraph**, sign manual or flourish of the ruler, appearing on stamps of Turkey (1863–1908), Hejaz-Nejd (1926–32), Afghanistan (1927–8) and Saudi Arabia (1932–45) as a mark of authority.

Toughra (Turkey, 1901, 1916)

TOURIST PUBLICITY STAMPS. Newfoundland (1897) and New Zealand (1898) pioneered the issue of stamps depicting places of scenic interest while France has pursued a deliberate policy of featuring tourist resorts on the higher denominations of definitive sets since 1929. France also pioneered the use of **slogan postmarks** advertising tourism. Belgium, Germany and Austria have made prolific use of handstamps for the same purpose. Many countries, notably Czechoslovakia, Switzerland and Austria, have issued lengthy sets of stamped postcards with scenic views. Australia has also issued picture postcards whose impressed stamps reproduce the scenes shown on the picture side. Britain experimented briefly with tourist aerogrammes (1963–4), but Scotland alone has persevered with this medium. Tourist aerogrammes have also been widely used by many other countries in recent years.

Tourist Publicity Stamps

Tourist Publicity Stamps

TRAFFIC LIGHTS. Term used by collectors to denote the check dots or colour dabs (to use the printers' jargon) printed in the sheet margins of stamps printed by modern offset litho or photogravure methods. They assist in checking that all the colours have printed correctly. Blocks of stamps from the corner of the sheet including the "traffic lights" are collected as a matched pair with the block showing the cylinder numbers. ■

TRAKBACK. A service of the British Post Office, introduced in 1986 as a more sophisticated form of **receipted parcel** service. Distinctive labels are employed, with **serial numbers** and **barcodes** which enable details of any parcel to be traced subsequently through computerised records.

TRANSFER. In lithography, the image laid down on the stone and built up to form the printing plate. If this is done carelessly it may result in a creased transfer, producing distortion in part of the impression or the lettering of the stamps.

TRANSFER ROLLER. In intaglio, the steel roller which transfers the image from the master die to the plate, using the "rocking-in" technique.

Trakback—British Post Office label

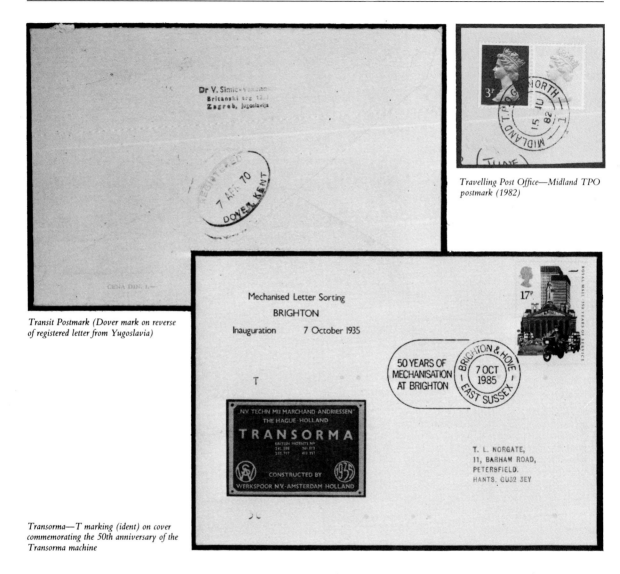

Travelling Post Office—Midland TPO postmark (1982)

Transit Postmark (Dover mark on reverse of registered letter from Yugoslavia)

Transorma—T marking (ident) on cover commemorating the 50th anniversary of the Transorma machine

TRANSIT POSTMARK. A postmark applied to a piece of postal matter at some point in its transmission between the office of collection and the office of delivery. At one time postmarks were applied to the backs of covers at all transit points, but this practice gradually died out in Britain from 1860 onwards, being at first restricted to the parent post offices to which the collection and delivery offices were subordinate, and then, from about 1895, to offices to which mail was missent or incorrectly routed. Transit marks may also be found to this day on international mail, the marks being applied at the offices of exchange (i.e. those offices handling incoming and outgoing mail by sea or air).

TRANSORMA. A machine for sorting incoming mail for street delivery, invented by J. Marchand and constructed by Professor J.C. Andriessen of Delft Technical College, Holland. It derived its name from Transportation and Sorting by Marchand and Andriessen. It was first demonstrated at the

International Aero-Postal Conference at the Hague (1927) and installed at Rotterdam head post office (1929). The Transorma machine was first used outside Holland in 1935, when two machines were installed in the Brighton and Hove sorting office, England. Each machine had five keyboards and was capable of sorting 24000 letters an hour. Mail sorted by Transorma received a mark consisting of a letter of the alphabet or numerals from 2 to 35. These Transorma markings may be found on items of mail addressed to the Brighton area, until July 1968 when they were withdrawn from use. Many different varieties of Transorma marking were employed and are now of great interest to students of postal mechanisation.

TRAVELLING POST OFFICE. A facility for posting and sorting mail aboard special railway trains, in order to accelerate mail-handling. Mail was first carried unofficially by rail in 1830 and officially in 1837. From January 1838 on-board sorting was adopted in England and gradually spread to other countries having a railway system. Special postmarks are used on TPOs to indicate mail posted in **late fee** posting boxes, or on the trains themselves. The postmarks may be recognised by two or more names indicating the termini of the route, wagon, train or route numbers, words such as "Up" or "Down" denoting the direction of the train, "Night" or "Day", the words "Sorting Carriage", "Sorting Tender", "Railway Post Office" or "Travelling Post Office", or their abbreviations. Equivalents in other languages include "Zug" (train), "Ambulant" (moving), or "Fahrendes Postamt". *See also* Highway Post Office.

TREASURY ESSAY. A proposed stamp design submitted in 1839 to the competition organised by the British Treasury to find the most practical means of putting Rowland Hill's postal reforms into effect. Over 2600 entries were received and four prizes of £100 were awarded, although none of the prize-winning entries was subsequently used for the postage stamps of 1840.

TREASURY ROULETTE. Also known as a Gladstone roulette, from W.E. Gladstone, Chancellor of the Exchequer at the time, it was an experimental form of separation tested under the auspices of the Treasury in 1853–4, prior to the adoption of **perforation**.

TREATY PORTS. Certain Chinese seaports where the European powers were permitted trading facilities following a series of treaties from 1843 onwards. Britain had post offices or postal agencies in Amoy, Canton, Chefoo, Foochow, Hankow, Hoihow, Ningpo, Shanghai, Swatow and Tientsin which continued to operate until 1922. France, Germany, Russia, Italy, Japan and the United States also operated postal services in the Treaty Ports, many of which also had local stamps for municipal postal services. The various powers issued stamps suitably overprinted for use in their postal services.

Treaty Ports—Shanghai Municipality stamp

Trimmed

TRIMMED. Term denoting adhesive stamps whose perforations have been clipped, owing to faulty guillotining of **booklet panes** or **coils**. It is also used to describe the conversion of fiscal stamps to postal use by cutting off a portion of their design, e.g. India (1886), Macao (1887), Ecuador (1892), French Indian Settlements (1903) and Sonora, Mexico (1913).

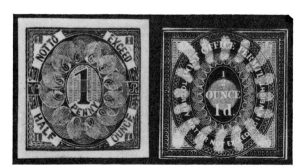

Treasury Essays

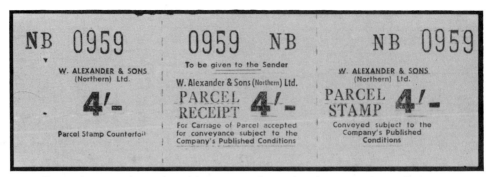

Tripartite Stamp—parcel stamp of Scottish bus company—reference stub, sender's receipt and stamp affixed to parcel

Triptych

TRIPARTITE STAMPS AND LABELS. Stamps issued by many bus and freight companies are printed in three parts, divided by **perforation** or **rouletting**. The left-hand portion is usually retained by the parcel clerk as a record of the transaction, the middle portion is affixed to the parcel, while the right-hand portion is kept by the sender as a receipt. Labels in three parts include those used by many postal authorities on overseas parcels. The two smaller portions, each bearing the parcel origin number, are affixed to the parcel and its accompanying documentation respectively, while the third and largest portion is retained as the sender's receipt. The British Post Office experimented in 1972–3 with tripartite registration labels, confined to Scotland, two portions being used to sim-plify the hand-to-hand check in transit and the third remaining on the registered packet to its destination.

TRIPTYCH. Group of three different stamps printed side by side in the sheet. South West Africa has issued sets of stamps (1968 and 1978) inscribed in English, German and Afrikaans respectively. Many **composite stamps** are produced in strips of three or more, side by side. St Lucia's Easter series of 1970 actually reproduced the Hogarth Triptych and not only spread this over three stamps but simulated the staggered effect of the original by having the side stamps positioned lower in the sheet than the centre stamp.

Two-Tier Post—GB first and second class postmarks (with and without time)

TWO-TIER POST. A postal service operating at two distinct levels, and offering two separate tariffs. Until 1870 the British Post Office did not offer any postage cheaper than the basic letter rate of a penny, but many other countries offered cheaper rates for printed matter and local mail. From 1870 to 1968 Britain operated a differential between letter post and printed matter (including circulars, samples, commercial papers, newspapers and periodicals). Since 1968 all categories of mail have been handled irrespective of their description, but the first- and second-class rates determine the speed at which they are handled and delivered. The principal philatelic effect of the two-tier system may be seen in the **phosphor** bands, one band appearing on those stamps intended specifically for second-class mail. Other manifestations of it are to be found in machine cancellations and postage paid impressions. Postmarks for first-class mail include clock-time, whereas those for second-class mail usually show the date of cancellation only.

TYPESET. A design made up entirely of printer's type, rule and ornaments, as opposed to one which incorporates a design drawn or engraved for the purpose. The essays produced by James Chalmers in 1838 to illustrate his proposals for uniform postage were printed from movable type, but the first actual stamps produced by this method were the British Guiana "Cottonreels" of 1850–1. British Guiana favoured typeset stamps as late as 1882. Other notable examples include the Hawaiian "Missionaries" (1851–2) and early issues of Reunion (1852), Soruth (1867–8), Mexico (1867), Fiji (1870), Nawanagar (1877), Guadeloupe (1878–84) and various Colombian states (1883–1902). Typeset postage due labels have been issued by Baden (1862), Malta (1925) and St Lucia (1930). Typeset inscriptions are, of course, commonly met with in **overprints** and **surcharges**.

Typeset (Surinam, Guadeloupe, Malta)

Typewritten Overprint (Tonga, ½d. on 7½d. on 2.)

TYPEWRITTEN OVERPRINTS AND SURCHARGES. Inscriptions produced by typewriting to alter the purpose or value of stamps. Overprints include those used in Colombia (1920) and Nicaragua (1929) to convert ordinary stamps to airmail use. Indian stamps were overprinted by typewriting for use in Pakistan (1947). Surcharges applied by typewriting include those issued in Tonga (1896), Thailand (1902) and Long Island (1916).

TYPEWRITTEN STAMPS. Stamps produced by typewriting date from 1894 when a local stamp was produced by Cuthbert Brothers of Belize for the Caye Service. The first stamps of Uganda (1895–6) were typeritten by the Rev. Ernest Miller at Mengo. Later stamps produced entirely by typewriting include Ermelo and Carolina guerrilla stamps (1900), Albania (1913–15), Long Island (1916), and German postwar provisionals of Bad Saarow and Eckartsberga (1945).

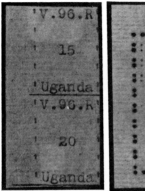

Typewritten Stamps (Uganda, 1895–6; Long Island, 1916)

TYPOGRAPHY. The style, arrangement or appearance of typeset matter, but loosely used by philatelists to denote the Letterpress process.

Typography

UNAPPROPRIATED DIES. The popular name for British **fiscal stamps** officially described as the unappropriated duty stamps, from the fact that space was provided in their designs for the overprint of the duty, or purpose, for which they were specifically intended. These fiscal stamps were produced by De La Rue for the Stamping Branch of the Inland Revenue at Somerset House and were the fiscal counterpart of the keyplate postage stamps of many British colonies. There were three basic designs, the duties being applied by a second printing. The unappropriated dies were also used for the **Military Telegraph stamps** of 1885 and the postage stamps of British Bechuanaland (1887).

Unappropriated Dies used on for GB revenue issues

UNDELIVERABLE MAIL. Mail which cannot be delivered because the addressee is dead, gone away without leaving a forwarding address or otherwise unknown to the delivery office, or because the address given is insufficient, illegible or incorrect. Such mail is usually returned to the sender endorsed with an explanation, or bearing adhesive labels to the same effect. Many countries have, or had, a wide range of labels for this purpose, often inscribed in French as well as the indigenous language, while the British Post Office until recently preferred **explanatory marks** but now uses a multi-purpose label, the reason for non-delivery being indicated by ticking the appropriate box. *See also* Returned Letter Stamps and Returned Mail.

THIS LETTER FORMED PART OF UNDELIVERED MAILS WHICH FELL INTO THE HANDS OF THE ALLIED FORCES IN GERMANY. IT IS UNDELIVERABLE AS ADDRESSED, AND IS THEREFORE RETURNED TO YOU.

Royal Mail
Undelivered for reason stated – return to sender

Gone away ☐	Not known at No ☐	
Not addressed ☐	Incomplete address ☐	
Refused ☐	Not called for ☐	
No answer ☐	Deceased ☐	
No such street/place in		

Duty No   Date
Initials
P 3960

Undeliverable Mail Marking and British Post Office label

appropriate surcharge. More recently Hungary (1946) and China (1949) overprinted stamps to denote their duty, during periods of hyper-inflation. US Christmas stamps (1975) were issued undenominated due to imminent but undetermined increases in postal rates. Subsequently the USA has issued undenominated definitive stamps, coded A, B, C or D (1978–85), for use on domestic mail when postal rate increases were again imminent. Canada adopted a similar principle in 1982. Sweden has issued undenominated stamps since 1979 inscribed INRIKES POST (inland mail) for sale to customers at a **discount**. British postal stationery since 1982 has gradually switched to an undenominated policy, beginning with postnotes of that year, then first- and second-class envelopes (1984), aerogrammes and registered envelopes (1986). ∎

UNDERPRINT. A tint or feint pattern underlying the main design of a stamp, and usually applied as a security measure to render forgery difficult or prevent cleaning off the postmark. Examples include the parcel stamps of the North German Confederation (1867) with the value in minuscule lettering continuously repeated, and many issues of Estonia and Latvia with a pattern of burelage. *See also* Moiré, and Winchester Paper. The term is also loosely applied to stamps which have **printed** matter **on** the **back**.

UNEMPLOYED INTELLECTUALS STAMPS. Stamps issued by France between 1935 and 1940 with a premium in aid of dole money for unemployed intellectuals. Hungary issued similar stamps in 1940 on behalf of unemployed artists.

Unemployed Intellectuals Stamp (France, 1935–40)

UNDENOMINATED STAMPS. Stamps which do not show an actual face value. Several British colonies in the 1850s issued such stamps, using different colours to indicate the value and thus save the cost of preparing different plates for each value. In this category come the stamps of Trinidad (1851–79), Barbados (1852–73), Mauritius (1858–62), the Ionian Islands (1859–64) and St Helena (1863–84), the last named actually being denominated 6d but printed in different colours with an

UNGUMMED STAMPS. The majority of stamps are provided with adhesive on the back so that they may be affixed to correspondence and so perform their postal function. Unused stamps may be ungummed because they have stuck together and have had to be soaked apart. Stamps have been officially issued without gum in countries which have a hot, humid climate. In such cases gum-pots are usually provided at post office counters for customers to affix stamps to their mail.

Among the countries which have issued ungummed stamps are China, Japan, Korea, North Vietnam, Taiwan, Surinam and Brazil. The typewritten stamps of Uganda and Long Island were also issued ungummed; in the former case adhesive was provided by tree resin while in the latter case flour and water paste was used.

UNISSUED STAMPS. Those which have been officially prepared, but for some reason have not been issued for postal use. When they are actually listed in catalogues they are usually described as "Prepared for use but not issued". There are many reasons for this: an error in design or inscription detected prior to release, or a sudden change of political regime are the most likely causes. Sometimes stamps are not issued for operational reasons, such as a sudden change in postal rates which renders the issue superfluous.

Unissued Stamps (Haiti, Mauritius)

UNIVERSAL COLOURS. *See* Postal Union Colours.

Ungummed Stamps (Brazil (adhesive paper, no apparent gum), China, North Vietnam, North Korea, Japan, Surinam)

Universal Postal Union—75th anniversary and centenary stamps

UNIVERSAL POSTAL UNION. Otherwise known as the *Union Postale Universelle* or UPU, it is a supranational body rationalising postal co-operation between the different countries of the world. It was mooted by Montgomery Blair of the USA in 1863 but not actually founded by Heinrich von Stephan of Prussia till 1874, and has its headquarters in Berne, Switzerland. Its various conferences, held since 1874, have adopted important decisions governing both inland and overseas mail. For example, compensation for loss of registered packets and the use of registration labels were decisions of the Paris conference (1878), international reply coupons (Rome 1906), metered mail (Madrid, 1920), Customs green labels for small packets (Stockholm, 1924) and aerogrammes (Paris, 1947). Many countries issued stamps in 1949 and 1974 to celebrate the 75th anniversary and the centenary of the UPU respectively.

UNOFFICIAL LABELS. *See* Private Labels.

UNOFFICIAL STAMPS. Stamps issued by bus, airline and shipping companies, carriers and freight companies to prepay the charges on their parcels and packets. Although such services may be sanctioned officially they have no official validity. *See also* Local stamps.

Unusual Perforation (Queensland 'Combination' perforation)

UNUSED. The term signifying that a stamp has not been used in the post and is consequently not postmarked or otherwise defaced, though it may be partially or wholly without gum or have been so heavily or frequently hinged as no longer to be regarded as mint.

USED. A stamp which has had postal, telegraphic or fiscal use and has been cancelled accordingly. "Fine used" implies that the postmark is light but sharp and clear, and that a sufficient proportion of it appears on the stamp to facilitate identification (and preferably the date of use), although this is not an essential qualification.

Unofficial Stamps—GB West Country Air Services (1930s)

UNMOUNTED MINT. Stamps in pristine condition, as issued from the post office, and which have never been hinged or mounted in any way. Such stamps tend to command a premium over **mounted mint** or **unused** stamps.

UNUSUAL PERFORATIONS. Perforation that differs from the conventional types in some way. Thus some early Queensland stamps were perforated by square holes combined with round holes and pin roulette, while the first Bulgarian postage due labels were perforated by lozenge-shaped holes. Some Australian coil stamps have a special perforation of large and small holes, intended to facilitate separation when withdrawing the stamps from vending machines. Some modern stamps of Mexico also have alternate large and small holes, and the first issues of Bussahir have large holes, gauging between 7 and 11.5, made by a type of fitted sewing-machine.

Used—fine used stamps of Singapore and USA

USED ABROAD. The stamps of one country used and postmarked in another country. Post offices, postal agencies and consular posts were established by the major European powers in the less-developed parts of the world and though they gradually died out after the foundation of the Universal Postal Union in 1874 they survived in some cases as late as the 1960s. In many instances stamps were specially overprinted and/or surcharged for this purpose, but others, particularly in the 19th century, were not distinguished in any way from those of the mother country, apart from the cancellation. Ordinary British stamps were used in many foreign countries, from Argentina (1860) to Egypt (1882), and in colonies from the 1850s till 1952 (Tristan da Cunha). French stamps were similarly widely used as late as 1931 (Egypt), as were the stamps of Austria, Russia, Germany, the United States and Australia in various places at various times.

Used Abroad (GB in Suez)

USED FISCALLY. Postage stamps, or more usually stamps inscribed "postage and revenue", used for the payment of revenue charges, such as receipts, cheque endorsement and stamp duty on legal documents and bills. They can invariably be distinguished from postal usage by the cancellation - either in manuscript or by the colour, type and wording of the cancellation. In some cases the stamps may also have been overprinted by a local authority as a security measure, making their fiscal purpose obvious.

Used Fiscally

USED ON COVER OR ENTIRE. Stamps postmarked and preserved on the original envelope, wrapper or postcard. Desirable in the case of early stamps, especially with interesting, unusual or rare cancellations, **backstamps** and **transit marks** or evidence of unusual handling, e.g. pioneer flights, **campaign covers** and on **travelling post offices**.

Used on Cover

USED ON PIECE. A stamp retained on a portion of the original cover or card to preserve the entire postmark.

Used on Piece (GB used in Malta)

Used Proofs (Italy 5c. in brown)

USED PROOFS. Proofs which have subsequently performed postal duty. Trial printings of Lithuania's National Assembly stamps of 1920 were made available from post offices for the prepayment of postage. Occasionally proofs of other countries' stamps have been irregularly used on mail, but gone through the post without detection.

V LABELS. Serial labels, similar to registration labels but having the letter V (from French *Valeur* = value) instead of the usual prominent R, and often printed in red ink, or on red-tinted paper. These labels are employed on insured letters, packets and parcels.

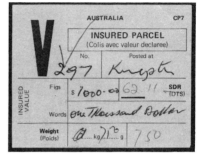

V Label (Australia, 1986)

V MAIL. Inscription on special forms and envelopes used by the US forces during the Second World War for a service analogous to the British forces' **airgraph** service.

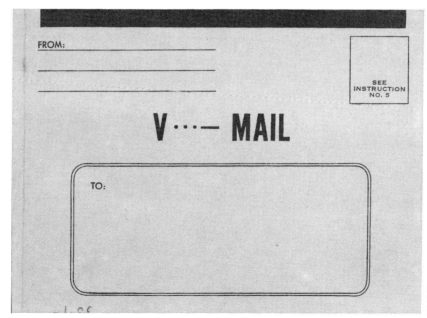

V Mail—used by US forces in Second World War

VALE. Spanish word meaning "worth" or "valid", overprinted on railway stamps of Nicaragua (1911) to convert them for postal use.

Vale (Nicaragua, 1911, railway stamp surcharged for fiscal then postal use)

VALUE CONVERTED. When Mexican paper currency depreciated in value in 1916–18, various stamps were overprinted with a device signifying that the face value was raised to par with the new "infalsificable" paper money. ∎

VALUE ERASED. The denomination erased from a printing plate in order that new values can be created by printing in different colours. This device was used by the Argentinian state of Corrientes (1860–80). ∎

VALUE INSERTED. Stamps printed without specific values, these being inserted by means of handstamp or manuscript prior to issue. The typeset provisional issues of Barbacoas, Colombia (1901–3) had the value and date of issue inserted in manuscript, while stamps of Albania (1913) had the values inserted by typewriting. ∎

VALUE TABLET. The panel or space on a stamp carrying the declared monetary value.

Value tablet—value in octagonal-shaped tablet

VARIETY. A stamp differing in some visible detail of its manufacture from the normal issue, caused by a fault in the printing process. Errors of colour, design, **perforation** and **watermark** are also sometimes loosely termed "varieties". The term is properly used to denote machine faults on specific stamps, which range from the comparatively insignificant or minor **flaw** having little more than curiosity value or transient interest, to the most striking and/or rare fault, such as a missing colour which can dramatically alter the appearance of a stamp. Types of variety will be found under Albino, Broken Letters, Capped Numerals, Clipped Transfer, Colour Changeling, Cracked Plate, Creased Transfer. Decoupage, Double Letters, Dropped Letters, Dry Print, Hand-painted, Inking Faults, Inserted by Hand. Ivory Head, Misplaced, Mixed Type, Palimpsest, Part Impression, Part Perforation, Printing Flaws, Re-entry. Retouch, Reversed Print, Set-off, Setting Error, Slurred and Smudged Prints and Worn Plate.

VARNISH LINES. Bars of varnish applied across the face of stamps issued by Austria (1901–7) to hinder cleaning and re-use. Three different widths of diagonal line were applied. ∎

VENDING MACHINE STAMPS. Stamps designed or printed specially for sale in coin-operated slot machines. These may differ from ordinary stamps by being imperforate on two opposite sides, or by having some kind of perforation not encountered in stamps from normal sheets. In some cases in recent years countries which normally issue large-format pictorial definitives, have had to produce small-format stamps for sale in vending machines, e.g. Gibraltar for coils (1971) and booklets (1981) sold in vending machines, St Lucia (1973–6) and New Zealand (1978). *See also* Automatic Stamps and Frama Labels.

Vending Machine Stamp (New Zealand)

VERVELLE. Name given to a distinctive shade of the French 1 franc stamp of 1851, after the philatelist who discovered a sheet of this variety among the personal papers of Anatole Hulot, the eccentric superintendent of the government printing works where the stamps had been produced. The Vervelle stamps are much lighter in shade, due to their not having been gummed.

VIGNETTE. A picture that shades off gradually into the surrounding background. In philately it describes the pictorial motif in general, but ought to apply more specifically to those motifs that shade off imperceptibly in order to conceal any slight mis-alignment or lack of registration in bicoloured stamps such as the letterpress and intaglio pictorials of many French and British colonies respectively in the first half of the 20th century. The term has also been debased, however, in its country of origin, and French collectors now use it as a synonym for a pictorial label of no postal validity.

Vignette—sailing boat on Papua stamp, 1908

WAR STAMPS. Stamps issued under wartime conditions and so designated or inscribed, e.g. the issues of the various factions during the Mexican and Spanish civil wars. It may also be applied to the various War Effort propaganda issues of Canada and South Africa (1942).

War Stamps

WAR TAX STAMPS. Stamps inscribed or overprinted WAR, WAR TAX or WAR STAMP, sometimes incorporating a Red Cross, issued to raise money in wartime, usually over and above the normal postal charges. Spain pioneered these stamps in 1874 with an issue inscribed IMPUESTO DE GUERRA. Their use was compulsory on all mail, the money being used for the conduct of the Carlist Wars. War tax stamps were again issued in 1898 during the Spanish-American War.

The idea was revived in the British Empire in 1915, Canada and many colonies issuing stamps thus inscribed or overprinted until 1918. Outside the Commonwealth, only Liberia issued war tax stamps (1918) and none was issued during the Second World War.

War Tax Stamps

WATERMARK. A design, device or pattern in paper, generally visible by transmitted light, formed by the **dandy roll** at the wet pulp stage of manufacture, in which the pressure of the attached bits results in a thinning of the paper. The watermark may serve to identify the paper-maker, but is usually incorporated in the paper used for stamps as a security measure, to defeat the forger. With more sophisticated printing methods in recent years the use of watermarks is dying out. British stamps ceased to use them in 1967. *See* All-over Watermark, Gum Device, Impressed, Inverted, Marginal, Multiple, Overall Multiple, Paper-maker's, Printed, Sideways, Single and Stitch Watermark.

WATERMARK ERROR. Stamps may be found with part or all of the watermark missing due to a broken or missing bit - the shaped metal design of the watermark impressed in the paper pulp during manufacture. The Emblems watermark used for British stamps (1856-67) normally had two roses, a thistle and a shamrock in the corners, but errors are known with three roses and a shamrock or thistle. In the Large Crown watermark used in 1854-64 two crowns of entirely different shape are found in certain sheets. The Multiple Crown Script CA watermark used for colonial stamps is known in 1950-2 with a crown missing, and later with a St Edward's crown inserted by mistake to fill the gap. Watermarks may also be found inverted, reversed, or inverted and reversed, although in the case of some **booklet** stamps inversion may be normal, just as **sideways watermarks** may be normal in **coils**.

Watermark Error (GB Penny Red inverted crown, George V ½d. missing crown)

WINCHESTER PAPER. A highly distinctive type of security paper with an underprinted pattern to prevent re-use and forgery. It was used for the 1932 airmail series of Venezuela.

WING MARGIN. An extra wing or extension of the margin forming part of the stamp, caused in British letterpress stamps produced by De La Rue when the vertical gutters of sheets were perforated centrally instead of close to the divided stamps. Collectors should beware of wing margin stamps which have had the margin trimmed close - a bad habit of 19th century collectors who did this to fit their stamps into the spaces provided for them in printed albums - or, even worse, trimmed stamps which have been re-perforated to conceal the original vandalism. Such re-perforation can, of course, be detected because of the **check letters** in the corners of the stamps, their sequence identifying stamps from the rows adjoining the gutters.

Wing Margin

WORN PLATE. A printing plate which, through constant usage, is showing extensive signs of wear. The stamps printed from such a plate will show blurred lines (especially in the letterpress process), while stamps from a worn intaglio plate are generally much lighter in appearance, as the worn grooves and recesses do not pick up as much ink as formerly. British line engraved stamps provide numerous examples, but the most notable may be found among the Penny Universal stamps of New Zealand. ∎

WOVE PAPER. The normal type of paper used for printing stamps, having in its texture the plain mesh of a fine wire-gauze sieve or mould, as opposed to **laid paper**.

Wove Paper (Belgium, Bahamas)

WRECK COVER. An item of mail which has been salvaged from a shipwreck. Such covers, often exhibiting stains and other evidence of immersion in sea water, are usually endorsed in manuscript, handstamp or by means of an adhesive label by the postal authorities to explain their condition. The earliest example of shipwrecked mail being specially marked was in 1846 when letters saved from the wreck of the Great Liverpool were thus marked with a framed handstamp. Items salvaged from disasters involving mail-trains and aircraft are usually termed **Crash covers**.

> **SALVED FROM**
> **S.S. "LEINSTER".**

Wreck Cover—marking used on mail recovered from SS Leinster

XYLOGRAPHY. The art of engraving on wood. Some stamps of Victoria (1854–9) were true woodblocks, individually engraved to form a plate of 50 impressions. For the Registration and Too Late stamps, separate stereotyped plates for the secondary colours augmented the woodblocks, while in the Emblems series (1857–60) electrotyped plates were made from woodblock dies. ∎

ZEMSTVO POSTS. The name given to the services organised in the zemstvos (units of local government in rural Russia). The Russian imperial post only served the cities and major towns but in 1864 local authorities were permitted to establish networks of postal services in the rural areas and to connect them with the imperial posts. The first zemstvo post was established at Vetlonga (1864) but Schlusselburg issued the first stamps (1865). Greater freedom in stamp design was permitted from 1870 onwards and from then until 1917, when the last services were suppressed at the Revolution, several thousand different stamps were issued.

Zemstvo Posts—Russian local issue

Zigzag Roulette (Germany, Danzig, Epirus)

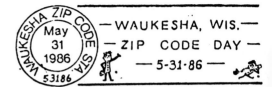

Zip Code—Mr Zip on postmark and in selvage

Zeppelin Post cover (1930)

ZEPPELIN POSTS. Airmail services operated in connexion with flights of German dirigible balloons between 1909, when the first postcards with distinctive cachets were produced, till 1937 when the ill-fated Hindenburg burst into flames while landing at Lakehurst, New Jersey. In the years immediately before the First World War Zeppelin airships made many demonstration flights, and souvenir cards, cachets and special postmarks were used. In the inter-war period, however, Zeppelins were used on international flights and many countries issued special stamps in connexion with the trans-Atlantic, polar and world flights.

ZIGZAG ROULETTE. Also known by the French term *percé en pointes*, this form of separation consists of short cuts at angles resulting in sharp pointed teeth along the edges of the stamps. It was used for stamps of La Guaira (1864) and Queensland (1899). It is similar to a **saw-tooth roulette**, though the points are smaller.

ZIP CODE. Postcode used in the USA, the name being derived from Zone Improvement Plan. It was introduced in July 1963. It consists of five digits, the first two identifying the state and the others identifying the town. To publicise the use of ZIP codes the USPO issued a 10c stamp in 1973, and has also used a cartoon character, Mr Zip to promote the system. Mr Zip is to be found with an appropriate slogan on many postmarks, as well as in the sheet margins of stamps and the coupons on booklet panes.